DATE DUE

6496
Metro Litho
Oak Forest, IL 60452

FEB 2 9 1888			

AMERICA the BEAUTIFUL

MARYLAND

By Deborah Kent

Consultants

Gregory A. Stiverson, Ph.D., Assistant State Archivist, Maryland State Archives

Robert L. Hillerich, Ph.D., Bowling Green State University, Bowling Green, Ohio

CHILDRENS PRESS®
CHICAGO

The Hooper Strait Lighthouse at the Chesapeake Bay Maritime Museum in St. Michaels

Project Editor: Joan Downing
Associate Editor: Shari Joffe
Design Director: Margrit Fiddle
Typesetting: Graphic Connections, Inc.
Engraving: Liberty Photoengraving

Library of Congress Cataloging-in-Publication Data

Kent, Deborah.
  America the beautiful. Maryland / by Deborah Kent.
    p.   cm.
  Summary: Introduces the geography, history,
government, economy, industry, culture, historic sites,
and famous people of the Old Line State.
    ISBN 0-516-00466-2
    1.   Maryland—Juvenile literature.
[1.   Maryland.]   I.   Title.
F181.3.K46   1990
975.2—dc20   89-25282
                                                    CIP
                                                     AC

The doorway of a colonial home along Cornhill Street in the Annapolis Historic District

TABLE OF CONTENTS

Chapter 1

MARYLAND, LAND IN THE MIDDLE

MARYLAND, LAND IN THE MIDDLE

"I can't win," Marylanders sometimes complain. "Down South they call me a Yankee, and up North they say I have a southern accent!" Maryland lies in a kind of buffer zone between Virginia, with its time-honored southern heritage, and the distinctly northern state of Pennsylvania. Marylanders speak with a soft, lilting drawl, and many parts of the state possess an air of southern charm. Yet Baltimore resembles industrial cities in Pennsylvania and New England, and Maryland's Washington, D.C., suburbs have a polish of northern sophistication.

Even the ecology of Maryland places it on the border between North and South. Near Oakland in Garrett County grow species of lichens and other plants that are typical of northern Canada. In Calvert County on Chesapeake Bay is found one of the nation's northernmost stands of bald cypresses.

Physically, eastern and western Maryland could hardly be more unlike each other. The flat, fertile Eastern Shore is dominated by the vast Chesapeake Bay. Fishing and boating are part of the region's way of life. Western Maryland, in contrast, is jagged with rocky hills. Its winding valleys harbor deep veins of coal.

Writer H. L. Mencken once remarked that Maryland would face extinction if its opposites were not so evenly matched. Yet northern and southern elements and eastern and western traditions continue to flourish. With all of their differences, as Mencken observed, Marylanders have had to learn a special tolerance. Perhaps it is this ability to tolerate differing and often conflicting characteristics that enables Maryland to keep its delicate balance as a state in the middle.

Chapter 2

THE LAND

THE LAND

GEOGRAPHY AND TOPOGRAPHY

On a map, the state of Maryland roughly resembles a revolver, its muzzle pointing westward into the Appalachian Mountains. Western Maryland is very narrow in places, measuring only 2 miles (3.2 kilometers) across at the town of Hancock. The stock of the revolver, eastern Maryland, is nearly cut in two by the vast Chesapeake Bay. With an area of 10,460 square miles (27,091 square kilometers), Maryland ranks forty-second in size among the states.

Although Maryland lies in the Southern Atlantic region of the United States, it has only 31 miles (50 kilometers) of Atlantic shoreline. The gentle curves of the Potomac River form Maryland's southern boundary with Virginia and West Virginia. A diamond-shaped sliver of land on the east bank of the Potomac was set aside nearly two centuries ago as the federal capital— Washington, District of Columbia. The West Virginia boundary line angles north to form Maryland's western tip. Maryland's northern border with Pennsylvania is sometimes called Mason and Dixon's Line. In the northeastern corner of Maryland, Mason and Dixon's Line cuts southward to mark the border with Delaware.

Geographers divide Maryland into five regions: the Appalachian Plateau, the Appalachian Ridge and Valley, the Blue Ridge, the Piedmont, and the Atlantic Coastal Plain. These regions

The Blue Ridge, a narrow strip of mountainous land in north-central Maryland

are portions of large topographical areas that run from northeast to southwest along the eastern coast of the United States.

Maryland's highest point, Backbone Mountain, stands 3,360 feet (1,024 meters) in the Appalachian Plateau region, a rugged triangle of land in the state's northwestern corner. East of this region lie a series of broad, fertile valleys divided by high ridges. This region, the Appalachian Ridge and Valley, extends from New Jersey to Alabama. In Maryland it includes the fertile Hagerstown Valley, noted for its farms and orchards. Beyond the Hagerstown Valley rises the scenic Blue Ridge, a band of mountains stretching from Pennsylvania to Georgia. South Mountain and Catoctin Mountain belong to Maryland's Blue Ridge section.

East of Catoctin Mountain, the land grows less rugged, sloping down to form a region of gently rolling hills called the Piedmont. Wheat, corn, oats, and many other crops grow in the fertile limestone soil.

Above: Autumn foliage near Grantsville in the
northwest corner of the state
Right: Farmland and an old church near Burkittsville

At the eastern edge of the Piedmont, the altitude drops sharply.
Many rivers tumble to the Atlantic Coastal Plain below in
foaming waterfalls. For this reason, the division between the
Piedmont and the coastal plain is called the Fall Line. In
Maryland, the Fall Line zigzags from Elkton in the north to the
Great Falls of the Potomac in the south.

More than half of Maryland's land area lies within the Atlantic
Coastal Plain (also called the Tidewater Plain), a smooth, fertile
region that runs from New Jersey to Florida. In Maryland, the
Chesapeake Bay cuts the coastal plain into two distinct sections,
the Western Shore and the Eastern Shore. Maryland's Eastern
Shore shares a broad peninsula with Delaware and a tiny
fragment of Virginia. This strip of land is named the Delmarva
Peninsula after the three states that comprise it.

Above: A woodland stream in the Appalachian Ridge and Valley region

Tobacco was once the mainstay of Maryland's coastal plain. Today, the region produces a wide variety of fruits and vegetables, as well as poultry and dairy cattle. Shipping, fishing, and tourism are vital ingredients to the region's economy. The Chesapeake has molded the character of eastern Maryland, where the water is never more than a few miles away.

THE CHESAPEAKE, GATEWAY TO THE SEA

To geologists, Chesapeake Bay is a "drowned riverbed." Thousands of years ago, the Susquehanna River flowed directly into the Atlantic. As the land gradually sank to form the Atlantic Coastal Plain, the ocean swept in and submerged much of the riverbed.

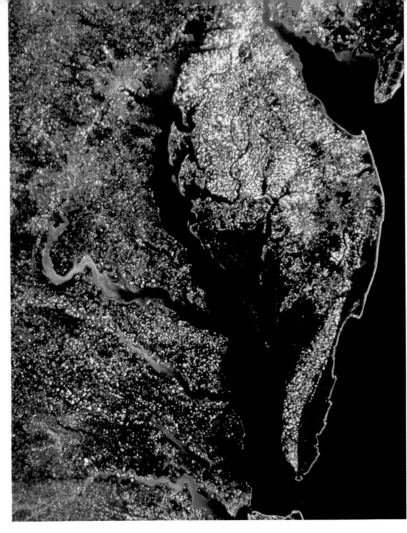

Chesapeake Bay, shown here in a photograph taken from a space satellite, is the largest inlet along the Atlantic coast of the United States.

Nearly 200 miles (322 kilometers) in length and more than 3,200 square miles (8,288 square kilometers) in area, the Chesapeake is the largest inlet along the Atlantic coast of the United States. A little more than half of the bay falls within Maryland's borders; its lower reaches are controlled by Virginia. The bay is jagged with marshy coves and jutting promontories, giving Maryland 3,190 miles (5,134 kilometers) of coastline. Since colonial days, the Chesapeake has served as an avenue for ships; a route from Maryland's interior to the Atlantic. Maryland's busiest seaports—Baltimore, Annapolis, and Cambridge—all face the bay.

In contrast, Maryland's tiny stretch of Atlantic coast offers no

The Potomac River, which forms the southern and southwestern boundaries of Maryland, is the state's longest river.

commercially valuable harbors. The mainland along the coast is sheltered by a series of sandy barrier islands. Assateague Island (the southern third of which belongs to Virginia) is an important wildlife refuge. The coastal town of Ocean City has developed into a major Atlantic coast resort.

RIVERS AND LAKES

Skirting the southern rim of the state, the Potomac is Maryland's largest and most important river. The headwaters of the Potomac's northern branch mark Maryland's southwestern corner. The Potomac winds for nearly 385 miles (620 kilometers) before it reaches Chesapeake Bay. At its mouth, the river is 12 miles (19 kilometers) wide and 45 feet (14 meters) deep. The Monocacy River is the Potomac's most important tributary in Maryland.

Man-made Deep Creek Lake, in Garrett County, is Maryland's largest lake.

Like the Potomac, most of Maryland's smaller rivers empty into Chesapeake Bay. Chief of these is the Susquehanna, which rises in New York and flows southward through Pennsylvania and Maryland's Cecil County. Rivers on the western side of the bay include the Severn, Gunpowder, Patapsco, and Patuxent. The Chester, Choptank, and Pocomoke feed the bay from the Eastern Shore. Several rivers and smaller streams in the Appalachian Plateau flow into the great Ohio River system, whose waters eventually reach the Mississippi River and the Gulf of Mexico. The largest of these is the scenic Youghiogheny, which flows north to join the Monongahela in Pennsylvania.

Though thousands of acres of wetlands lie along the Chesapeake, Maryland has few natural ponds or lakes. The largest lake in the state is man-made Deep Creek Lake in Garrett County. Covering 3,900 acres (1,578 hectares), Deep Creek Lake is a popular summer resort.

According to legend, Assateague Island's wild ponies are descendants of horses that swam ashore from a wrecked Spanish galleon in the 1500s.

PLANT AND ANIMAL LIFE

About 40 percent of Maryland's land, some 3 million acres (1.2 million hectares), is covered with forests. Spruce, hemlock, white pine, maple, and hickory trees grow in the mountains and on the Piedmont. Yellow pine, cedar, and red gum trees are common in southern Maryland, and cypresses grow in the wetlands along the bay.

White-tailed deer are plentiful in most rural areas of the state. Small mammals found in Maryland's woodlands include red foxes, gray foxes, raccoons, opossums, skunks, woodchucks, weasels, and cottontail rabbits. Muskrats were once trapped extensively in the wetlands for their glossy pelts. Among Maryland's rarer mammals are the Delmarva fox squirrel of the Eastern Shore and the wild ponies that graze on Assateague Island.

In spring, the woodlands are alive with songbirds, including the striking yellow-and-black Baltimore oriole, Maryland's state bird. The wetlands along Chesapeake Bay provide nesting grounds for thousands of ducks, including mallards, black ducks, and

17

Every year, thousands of tons of clams are harvested from Chesapeake Bay.

canvasbacks. As many as 3 million Canada geese winter along the bay each year. Protected by law from hunters, bald eagles are making a slow comeback.

The name *Chesapeake* comes from an Indian word meaning "great shellfish bay." Every year, thousands of tons of clams, oysters, and crabs are harvested from the bay, providing a living for hundreds of "watermen" and their families. Many species of fish are also caught in the bay, both by sports enthusiasts and commercial fishermen.

CLIMATE

Warmed by the Gulf Stream, eastern Maryland has a mild climate. Winter temperatures average 39 degrees Fahrenheit (4 degrees Celsius) along the Chesapeake, compared with 29 degrees Fahrenheit (minus 1.6 degrees Celsius) on the

Appalachian Plateau. During the summer, however, the
mountainous regions remain pleasantly cool, while the coastal
plain can become hot and humid. July temperatures average
68 degrees Fahrenheit (20 degrees Celsius) in the mountains and
75 degrees Fahrenheit (24 degrees Celsius) on the bay.

Despite its mild climate, Maryland can experience extremes of
temperature. On January 13, 1912, the mercury plunged to a
bone-chilling minus 40 degrees Fahrenheit (minus 40 degrees
Celsius) at Oakland in Garrett County. On July 10, 1936, the
people of Cumberland and Frederick experienced a sizzling
109 degrees Fahrenheit (43 degrees Celsius). In late summer,
tropical storms sometimes batter the coast. In 1972, Hurricane
Agnes uprooted trees, flattened beachfront cottages, and destroyed
millions of dollars' worth of property.

In general, however, Maryland is blessed with a pleasant
climate. As Father Andrew White, one of Maryland's first English
settlers, wrote in 1635, "[The air] is mild and gentle; not so hot as
Florida and Old Virginia, nor so cold as New England, but
between them both, having the good of each and the ill of
neither."

19

Chapter 3
THE PEOPLE

THE PEOPLE

Mary Elizabeth Ames is the fastest crab picker in Crisfield.
Every day through the long summer months of crab season, she
works her way through heaps of steamed hard-shells, deftly
removing the tasty meat. Crab picking on Maryland's Eastern
Shore is a job that traditionally has been performed by women. It
is highly skilled work, and no machine is as efficient as the hands
of an experienced human picker.

Marylanders come from the wetlands of the Eastern Shore, from
sprawling suburbs, from teeming cities, and from remote
communities in the mountains. Whatever their background, they
all contribute their skills and ideas to build this diverse state.

POPULATION

With 4,216,941 people according to the 1980 federal census,
Maryland ranks eighteenth in population among the states. It is
the fifth-most-densely-populated state in the nation, with
403 people per square mile (156 people per square kilometer). In
contrast, the United States as a whole averages only 67 people per
square mile (26 people per square kilometer). Four-fifths of all
Marylanders are urban dwellers, living in or near cities.

As early as 1959, an editorial in Baltimore's *Sun* proclaimed,
"Baltimore and Washington [D.C.] are reaching out for each other
like octopuses, sending out tentacles of freeways, sewage lines,
and industrial zones." Today, the suburbs of the two great cities
almost meet.

Marylanders engaged in two distinctly Maryland activities: crab picking and decoy carving

More than half of Maryland's people live in Baltimore and its suburbs or along a 40-mile (64-kilometer) corridor that links Baltimore to Washington, D.C. Baltimore (which natives pronounce "Bawlmer") is by far the state's largest city, with 786,741 people. Five other cities, all of them in the Baltimore-D.C. area, have populations that exceed 50,000: Silver Spring, Dundalk, Bethesda, Columbia, and Towson. Annapolis, the state capital, is a small city of about 32,000 that lies about 20 miles (32 kilometers) south of Baltimore.

Away from this teeming metropolitan area, the population thins dramatically. Southern Maryland is still chiefly devoted to agriculture, and the mountain regions are heavily forested. Though it is now connected to the rest of Maryland by the Chesapeake Bay Bridge, the Eastern Shore remains relatively isolated. Somerset and Caroline counties are the most sparsely populated counties in the state.

WHO ARE THE MARYLANDERS?

The names of such towns as Oxford, Cambridge, and Dorchester reflect the influence of Maryland's early English settlers. Today, however, people of English descent are a minority in Maryland. German surnames are frequent in the central and western counties. Polish, Irish, and Italian Americans live throughout the state. People of virtually every ethnic heritage on earth can be found in and around Baltimore and in the suburbs of Washington.

About 18 percent of all Marylanders are black. Black people comprise about 55 percent of Baltimore's total population. Many black families live in the rural areas of southern Maryland and on the Eastern Shore.

Maryland was founded on the principle of freedom of religion. In keeping with this tradition, people of all faiths live in the state today. Roman Catholics make up the single largest religious group in the state. Among the most well-established Protestant denominations are the Presbyterian, Lutheran, Episcopalian, Methodist, and Baptist churches. About 5 percent of Marylanders are Jewish.

MANY MARYLANDS

It is sometimes said that there are many Marylands. Baltimore has more in common with such major cities as New York and Philadelphia than it has with quiet farming communities 50 miles (80 kilometers) away. Southern Maryland, cradled between the Potomac and the bay, has the atmosphere of rural Virginia. The people of Montgomery and Prince Georges counties, many of them government employees, may identify more with Washington, D.C., than with Maryland. The people of

Built in 1675, Old Trinity Church in Church Creek is America's oldest Episcopal church still in active use.

Hagerstown and Cumberland complain that the rest of the state thinks Maryland ends in Frederick. And the Eastern Shore has tried five times to separate from Maryland and become its own state.

Despite these regional differences, Marylanders are surprisingly unified in their political views. Since the nineteenth century, the Democratic party has been a powerful force within the state. In the presidential election of 1980, Maryland was one of only six states that voted for Democrat Jimmy Carter instead of Republican Ronald Reagan.

Nevertheless, one of the best-known Maryland political figures of the late twentieth century was Republican Spiro T. Agnew. A Towson lawyer of Greek descent, Agnew became Baltimore County executive in an upset election in 1962. In 1966, he was elected governor of Maryland. When Richard Nixon ran for the presidency in 1968, he chose Agnew as his running mate. However, Agnew's political career was cut short in 1973, when he resigned from the vice-presidency after pleading "no contest" to a charge that he had accepted bribes.

Chapter 4

THE BEGINNING

THE BEGINNING

*In summer no place afforded more plenty of
sturgeon, nor in winter more abundance of
fowl. . . . In the small rivers all the year
there was good plenty of small fish, so
that with hooks those that would take pains
had always sufficient.*
—Captain John Smith, describing the land along Chesapeake
Bay, which he first explored in 1608

MARYLAND'S FIRST PEOPLE

When Europeans arrived in the 1600s, about three thousand
Native American people lived in the land we now call Maryland.
They were the descendants of Asian people who crossed the
Bering Strait into North America about fifteen thousand years
ago. The Pocomoke, Choptank, and Nanticoke were small groups
that lived on the Eastern Shore. The Anaco, Piscataway,
Yaocomaco, and Patuxent of southern Maryland belonged to the
large family of Algonquian-speaking tribes scattered throughout
eastern North America. The Algonquian tribes functioned as
distinct nations, but they were related by similar languages and
customs.

Most of these Chesapeake groups were relatively small,
numbering only a few hundred members. Families built long huts
of bent saplings covered with marsh grasses. The women planted
beans, squash, tobacco, and maize (corn). The men hunted deer
and other game and netted fish in the streams and rivers. Oysters
were a staple food, and great mounds of discarded shells often
remained long after a village was abandoned.

An early European depiction of a Susquehannock village

The Chesapeake tribes were dominated by their powerful neighbors, the Susquehannock, who lived to the north along the river named in their honor. One early colonist, George Alsop, described the Susquehannock as "the most noble and heroic nation of Indians that dwell upon the confines of America; the men being, for the most part, seven foot high . . . their voices large and hollow as ascending out of a cave; their behavior majestic, treading on earth with much pride and contempt."

THE COMING OF THE EUROPEANS

No one is certain when the Native Americans of Maryland met Europeans for the first time. Some historians believe that French traders began to buy furs from the Indians along the Chesapeake early in the 1500s. Italian explorer Giovanni da Verrazano may have paused at Chesapeake Bay on his way up the Atlantic coast in the 1520s. In 1570, a Spanish priest established a short-lived outpost on the bay and attempted to convert the Indians to Christianity.

In 1608, a band of Susquehannock greeted a tall English ship that sailed into Chesapeake Bay with Captain John Smith at the helm. Awed by the pale-skinned strangers and their great vessel, the Susquehannock hurried to the shore with gifts of furs, arrows, and tobacco pipes. John Smith wrote that he had trouble persuading the Indians that he and his followers were not gods.

With a land grant from the British Crown, John Smith helped found the Virginia Colony on the James River 100 miles (161 kilometers) south of Chesapeake Bay. In 1631, a Virginian named William Claiborne led a band of settlers to Kent Island off Maryland's Eastern Shore. Claiborne considered the Kent Island colony to be a northern extension of Virginia. The settlement soon boasted a busy trading post where the colonists bartered with the Indians for furs.

Meanwhile, far across the Atlantic, a British nobleman named George Calvert, the first Lord Baltimore, was petitioning King Charles I for permission to colonize the land north of the Potomac. Calvert died two months before his request was granted. The king gave the charter to the land along Chesapeake Bay and north of the Potomac River to the second Lord Baltimore, George Calvert's oldest son, Cecil. At the king's request, Cecil Calvert

The *Dove*, a replica of which (right) is anchored at St. Mary's City, was one of two ships that carried English settlers to Maryland in 1633.

named his future colony after King Charles's beloved wife, Henrietta Maria. He called it Maryland.

The Calverts were devout Roman Catholics. At that time, Catholics were persecuted in Protestant England. Cecil Calvert dreamed of founding a colony where Catholics and Protestants could live and work side by side in complete religious freedom. Searching for men and women who were willing to venture into the Maryland wilderness, he assembled a group of Protestants and Catholics, including two priests. Cecil Calvert was unable to make the journey himself, so he appointed his younger brother Leonard as the colony's first governor.

In late 1633, the colonists set sail for Maryland in two ships, the *Ark* and the *Dove*. It was a harrowing voyage. The ships became separated during a fierce storm, and the *Ark*'s passengers feared that their sister ship was lost. To their joy, they were reunited with the *Dove* in the West Indies, where both ships had stopped to take on supplies. Together they sailed north to the mouth of the Potomac.

A romanticized depiction of the passengers of the *Ark* and the *Dove* landing at St. Clements Island in 1634

On March 25, 1634, the *Ark* and the *Dove* anchored off St. Clements Island. The colonists clambered ashore to hear one of the priests deliver Mass. Standing before the assembled colonists, Leonard Calvert proclaimed that all Christians would be free to worship as they chose in Maryland.

The colonists soon found an excellent harbor some 15 miles (24 kilometers) up the St. Mary's River. Leonard Calvert bargained with the Yaocomaco Indians, exchanging axes, hoes, blankets, and other goods for a 30-mile (48-kilometer) strip of land. The Yaocomaco and most of the other Chesapeake tribes proved eager to ally themselves with the newcomers, who might protect them from their enemies, the Susquehannock. They gave the settlers huts to live in and fields already planted with corn. Indian women taught the English women how to make cornmeal bread.

Inside a sturdy log fence, or palisade, the colonists built houses and a church. Although the settlement was tiny, they must have envisioned a glorious future, for they named it St. Mary's City.

THE GROWTH OF THE COLONY

Convinced that Kent Island belonged to Virginia, William Claiborne resisted Lord Baltimore's authority. In 1654, with the help of a group of Protestant settlers, Claiborne seized control of the Maryland Colony. He ruled it until 1658, when he was recalled to England. Maryland absorbed the Kent Island settlement, and Lord Baltimore regained control of the colony's government.

Little by little, the colonists spread onto the land that had once belonged to the Indians. Few of the Tidewater groups had the strength to resist. They had no natural immunities to smallpox and other diseases that the colonists had brought from Europe, and terrible epidemics ravaged their villages. The Susquehannock fought fiercely, attacking Kent Island and many of the outlying settlements. But they, too, were greatly weakened by disease. In 1652, the Susquehannock signed a treaty that gave their land on the upper Chesapeake to the Maryland Colony.

In 1649, Maryland passed a law officially stating the colony's policy of religious tolerance for all Christians. Encouraged by the new law, a group of Puritans fled into Maryland from Virginia, where they had been persecuted for their religious beliefs. They founded a settlement called Providence on the Severn River. Later, another settlement, named Anne Arundel Town in honor of Lord Baltimore's wife, was established on the other side of the river. In 1691, the Calverts lost control of Maryland, and it became a colony ruled directly by the British Crown. Three years later, the colonial governor, Francis Nicholson, moved the capital from

Annapolis, Maryland's capital, still retains the radiating street plan designed by Royal Governor Francis Nicholson in 1696.

St. Mary's City to Anne Arundel Town. He laid out the new capital in a series of circles and radiating streets and renamed it Annapolis in honor of Queen Anne. The Calverts regained control of Maryland in 1715.

In 1729, the colonial assembly established a town, called Baltimore, on the Patapsco River. The site offered an excellent harbor. Rich farmland lay to the west, and timber from nearby thick forests could fuel furnaces for smelting iron. Within two years, Baltimore was shipping grain and thick bars of pig iron to England.

Baltimore in 1752

During the 1730s, German colonists from Pennsylvania began to move onto land southwest of the Susquehanna River. Dispute over the ownership of this region led to some bloody confrontations between Marylanders and Pennsylvanians. In 1736, a Marylander named Thomas Cresap led his wife and a band of friends to a tract of land promised to him by the fifth Lord Baltimore. Cresap was determined to drive the Pennsylvanians from Maryland soil. Both the women and men of his party were well armed. Cresap's wife carried a rifle, two pistols, a tomahawk, and, in her boot, a dagger. After raiding several Pennsylvania German farms, Cresap was finally arrested and imprisoned in Philadelphia. According to legend, he once turned to one of his guards and declared, "Dammit, Aston, this is the prettiest town in Maryland!"

The dispute between Maryland and Pennsylvania was finally settled by two English surveyors, Charles Mason and Jeremiah

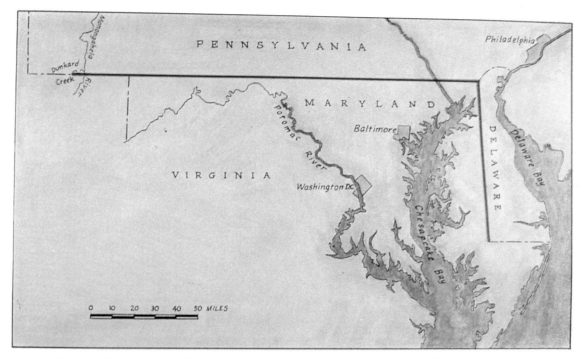

A map showing the boundary that became known as Mason and Dixon's Line

Dixon. For four years, from 1763 to 1767, they fought their way through the thick forests, marking a rigorously straight line between the two colonies. To this day, the boundary between Maryland and Pennsylvania is known as Mason and Dixon's Line.

German and Scotch-Irish farmers from Pennsylvania continued flocking to western Maryland. They cleared land in the fertile Antietam and Monocacy valleys, where they raised wheat, corn, and cattle. The villages of Frederick Town (later Frederick) and Elizabeth Town (later Hagerstown) grew up as trading centers for these scattered frontier settlements.

LIFE IN COLONIAL MARYLAND

The second Lord Baltimore and his heirs had proprietary control of the Maryland Colony. All of the land within the grant

St. Mary's City features a replica of a seventeenth-century tobacco plantation.

belonged to them. The lords proprietors also levied taxes and appointed public officials.

The second Lord Baltimore had viewed Maryland as a bold experiment in religious freedom. He also wanted the colony to turn a healthy profit. Virginia was successfully exporting tobacco, or "sot-weed," which had recently become popular in Europe. Lord Baltimore encouraged Maryland to do the same. In 1635, the Marylanders discovered that the sot-weed flourished in their rich Tidewater soil. Tobacco soon became so important to Maryland's economy that one settler called it "our meat, drink, clothing, and money."

After only three or four years, however, tobacco sapped the vital nitrogen and potash from the soil. Tobacco planters needed large landholdings in order to open up new fields when old ones were exhausted. By the 1650s, about 80 percent of the settled land in the colony had become part of large manors, or plantations.

In the early days, many of the plantation workers were bondmen, or indentured servants, from Great Britain. To pay for their passage to the colony, they sold themselves to a ship's captain, who in turn sold them to the planters for three to five years of servitude. They could be whipped for disobedience, and their period of bondage could double if they tried to run away.

The plantation workers labored twelve to fourteen hours a day, six days a week. According to one eyewitness, the houses provided by the landowners were "so wretchedly constructed that if you are not so close to the fire as almost to burn yourself you cannot keep warm, for the wind blows through them everywhere." Disease was rampant. About half of the people born in the colony died before the age of twenty. Smallpox, diphtheria, malaria, and dysentery took a heavy toll.

One of the original settlers who had come to Maryland on the *Ark* was a black servant named Mathias de Sousa. He later gained his freedom, and was the first black to sit in the Maryland General Assembly.

However, for the first fifty years of settlement, there were not many blacks in Maryland, and their legal status varied. Some were free, some were indentured servants, and some were slaves. In the 1680s, the supply of white indentured servants began to dry up. Planters quickly turned to African slaves to meet their labor needs.

Most Marylanders found that life was hard and the rewards were few. The vast majority lived in or near poverty their entire lives. By the 1700s, however, a few families had amassed large fortunes through shipping, iron manufacturing, land speculation, and other businesses. While their servants and slaves labored in the fields, these great planters lived in relative comfort. They built splendid homes and imported fine china and silver from France and England.

Annapolis quickly gained a reputation as a lively cultural center. Young ladies studied the harpsichord and other musical instruments, and professional musicians gave public concerts. In 1752, one of the the first theaters in the American colonies opened with a rollicking performance of John Gay's comedy *The Beggar's Opera.*

Unlike the Tidewater planters, the frontier farmers seldom could afford slaves or indentured servants. Most lived in simple one- or two-room log cabins. Corn was the mainstay of their diet. They cooked it into "hoecake" or "johnnycake," ground it into meal for porridge, and brewed it to make beer.

Culturally and economically, Maryland's Tidewater and Piedmont regions had little in common. For generations to come, these regional differences would color the way Marylanders felt about social and political issues.

THE ROAD TO INDEPENDENCE

In 1763, France and Great Britain signed a treaty that ended a long and bitter conflict known in North America as the French and Indian War. The British were victorious, but the war left the king's treasury nearly empty. The British Crown reasoned that the thirteen American colonies might be a valuable source of revenue. In 1765, the British Parliament passed the Stamp Act, the first of a series of taxes directed at the colonists.

The Stamp Act required the colonists to buy an official stamp whenever they purchased legal documents, newspapers, or even playing cards. Most Marylanders were outraged. One planter, Daniel Dulaney, Jr., wrote a pamphlet in which he argued that British subjects could not be taxed without their consent, and that the colonists could not give their consent because they had no

In several cities in the American colonies, including Annapolis, angry citizens protested the Stamp Act by hanging the local stamp distributor in effigy.

representatives in Parliament. Taking a more radical approach, a fiery young patriot named Samuel Chase led a mob through the streets of Annapolis, carrying the effigy of the local stamp distributor. The crowd cheered as the dummy was hanged and burned.

Similar protests throughout the colonies led to the repeal of the Stamp Act in 1766. But Parliament soon passed the Townshend Acts, a series of new taxes on such imported items as paint, glass, paper, and tea. Again the colonists rose in protest. In 1770, Parliament repealed the Townshend Acts, with the exception of the tax on tea.

In October 1774, the brig *Peggy Stewart*, loaded with 2,000 pounds (907 kilograms) of British tea, anchored in Annapolis Harbor. A band of Maryland patriots decided to prevent the tea from coming ashore. They forced the merchants who had ordered the tea and the ship's owner, Anthony Stewart, to sign a document confessing that they had ''committed a most daring insult to the liberties of America." Then they ordered Stewart to burn the ship's cargo. Instead, he set fire to the ship itself, and a crowd watched it burn to the waterline.

Many Marylanders deplored such violence, and hoped that the colony's differences with England could be resolved peacefully. One planter wrote that the burning of the *Peggy Stewart* "makes all men of property reflect with horror on their present situation. To have their lives and properties at the disposal and mercy of a mob is shocking indeed."

In April 1775, Maryland received word that British troops had fired on a band of colonial militiamen at Lexington, Massachusetts. Immediately, young men responded to the call to arms. On July 4, 1776, a year after the war began, three delegates from Maryland—Thomas Stone, William Paca, and John Rogers— voted for the Declaration of Independence in Philadelphia. The colonies had cut their ties to the mother country forever.

During the long and bloody Revolutionary War, no battles were fought on Maryland soil. Yet Maryland troops fought bravely far from their homes throughout the war. During the Battle of Long Island, Maryland soldiers held off the British while General George Washington and his army escaped to Manhattan. From the stubborn courage of its soldiers in the Continental Line during the Revolution, Maryland earned one of its nicknames, the Old Line State.

In an effort to keep supplies from reaching the rebellious colonies, British ships blockaded Chesapeake Bay during much of the war. Many Baltimore merchants armed their sloops and schooners and sent them to sea as "privateers." Swift and easy to maneuver among the bay's coves and inlets, the privateers mercilessly harassed British ships. During the course of the war, they captured hundreds of warships and merchant vessels,

The Treaty of Paris ending the Revolutionary War was signed in this chamber of the Maryland State House in 1784.

handing over much-needed food, clothing, and ammunition to the Americans.

From November 26, 1783, until August 13, 1784, Annapolis served as the nation's seat of government. On January 14, 1784, in the senate chamber of Maryland's State House in Annapolis, American leaders ratified the Treaty of Paris. The war was over, and the thirteen former colonies were independent at last. Yet debate raged over how the new nation should be governed and which city should serve as its capital.

In the summer of 1787, delegates from each of the new states met at a constitutional convention in Philadelphia to draft a body of laws for governing their nation. On April 28, 1788, Maryland became the seventh state to ratify the Constitution of the United States of America. Three years later, in 1791, Maryland donated nearly 70 square miles (181 square kilometers) of land on the Potomac to serve as the site of the nation's permanent capital — Washington, District of Columbia.

Chapter 5
GROWING WITH A NEW NATION

GROWING WITH A NEW NATION

On July 4, 1828, an excited crowd gathered at Mount Clare Plantation just outside Baltimore. As the spectators cheered, Charles Carroll of Carrollton helped to lay the first stone for the Baltimore and Ohio Railroad. At age ninety-one, Carroll was the only surviving signer of the Declaration of Independence. More than fifty years earlier, he had helped Maryland break its ties with Great Britain. Now he witnessed the dawn of a new era in Maryland—and in the country as a whole—an age of industry and invention.

WHAT SO PROUDLY WE HAILED

After the Revolutionary War, Baltimore became the fastest-growing city in the nation. Only New York, Philadelphia, and Boston were larger. Small ships, or packets, carried passengers and cargo from Baltimore to ports up and down the Atlantic coast. Larger vessels took tobacco and other goods to Europe and fetched cargo from the West Indies, South America, and even China.

British merchants resented the growing presence of American trading vessels, and tension mounted as the two nations vied for power on the high seas. In 1812, the hostilities flared into war.

During the War of 1812, Baltimore privateers once again marauded the seas, capturing more than five hundred British merchant ships. But unlike the Revolutionary War, which had left Maryland soil almost untouched, the War of 1812 threatened Marylanders at their very doorsteps.

In 1814, after defeating American troops in the Battle of Bladensburg,
British forces marched into Washington, D.C., and set the city ablaze.

In February 1813, British Admiral George Cockburn blockaded
the Chesapeake and greatly reduced shipping in and out of
Baltimore. Four months later, Cockburn raided the Chesapeake
port of Havre de Grace, looting homes and carrying away
furniture and other property. Cockburn's forces gathered on Kent
Island, while more British troops attacked towns on the Eastern
Shore.

In August 1814, Cockburn joined forces with a British army
detachment to rout the American militia at Bladensburg.
According to one observer, the half-trained American troops "ran
like sheep chased by dogs." With American resistance thrust
aside, the British marched into Washington, D.C., and set the city
ablaze.

Although Washington was the nation's capital, Baltimore was a
far more important commercial center. The British determined to
capture the city and destroy the shipyards that outfitted the hated

The sight of this American flag (top left) flying over Fort McHenry the day after the Battle of Baltimore (above) inspired Francis Scott Key (left) to write the famed anthem "The Star-Spangled Banner."

privateers. To defend their city, the men, women, and children of Baltimore worked feverishly with picks and shovels, erecting a line of earthwork fortifications from today's Patterson Park to the North Branch of the Patapsco River. The trenches and walls deterred the British from attacking the city by land. Instead, they decided to assail Fort McHenry, which guarded the city from Whetstone Point on the Patapsco.

Early on a September morning, sixteen British ships began to hurl bombs and rockets at Fort McHenry. The rockets were relatively harmless, though they crossed the sky in terrifying arcs of flame. The bombs were hollow iron spheres packed with gunpowder. When they landed, they exploded and scattered lethal fragments of razor-sharp metal. Often the bombs did not reach their target, but burst in midair.

Few Americans had seen such terrifying new weapons before. The noise was deafening, and the sky seemed to be on fire. Yet throughout the attack, an American flag flew defiantly above Fort McHenry. At last, after twenty-four hours of fighting, the fort's defenders drove off the British attack. Within a few more months, the war ended in an American victory.

One witness to the Battle of Baltimore was a Maryland-born lawyer named Francis Scott Key. Three days earlier, Key had boarded a British vessel to plead for the release of an American prisoner. Fearing that Key would reveal their plan to attack Fort McHenry, the British forced him to remain on shipboard.

From the deck, Key watched the raging battle. He spent the long night in an agony of doubt, fearing that Baltimore was lost. But as dawn broke, the smoke and haze cleared for a moment, and Key saw that the flag continued to fly over Fort McHenry. Thrilled with joy at the American triumph, he scribbled a few lines of poetry on the back of an envelope. That evening, after his release from the British ship, he completed a song that became popular almost overnight. Years later, in 1931, his song was selected as the national anthem of the United States. Today, Americans are stirred to pride in their nation's achievements when they hear the familiar opening lines of "The Star-Spangled Banner":

> Oh! say, can you see, by the dawn's early
> light,
> What so proudly we hailed at the twilight's
> last gleaming?

MARYLAND ON THE MOVE

Despite its prominence as a trading center, Maryland was at first hampered by a lack of adequate roads. In 1791, a visitor from France complained, "We saw ourselves confronted with abominable roads, where one runs the risk of being upset at any moment on sharp stones or of being thrown into mudholes." In 1787, the Maryland legislature authorized funds to launch an extensive road-building program. By the 1820s, several toll roads, or turnpikes, linked Baltimore with Frederick, Hagerstown, Williamsport, and other western Maryland towns. Macadam, a surface made from compacted layers of crushed gravel, was used for the first time on a road between Hagerstown and Boonsboro.

Thousands of settlers made their way to the western frontier along the National Road, which wound for 800 miles (1,287 kilometers) from Cumberland, Maryland, to Vandalia, Illinois. The most expensive project the federal government had undertaken up to that time, the National Road cost nearly $8 million to construct. Work on the road began in 1811 and was finally completed in 1852.

In 1824, construction began on the Chesapeake and Delaware Canal, a 13-mile (21-kilometer) waterway across the upper end of the Delmarva Peninsula. The canal gave Baltimore ships a shortcut to Delaware Bay and the Atlantic, sparing them the 200-mile (322-kilometer) journey down the Chesapeake. In 1828, Congress approved an even more impressive construction project, the Chesapeake and Ohio Canal, which would link Washington, D.C., on the Potomac with the Ohio River Valley. This feat of engineering had first been envisioned by George Washington decades before. Although never completed, by 1850 it stretched 184.5 miles (297 kilometers), to Cumberland in the western

Transportation in Maryland improved greatly in the early 1800s with the opening of the National Road (top), the Chesapeake and Ohio Canal (right), and the nation's first railroad, the Baltimore and Ohio (bottom).

mountains. An ingenious series of locks gradually lifted ships from sea level to an altitude of nearly 3,000 feet (914 meters).

Canals proved a boon to commerce in Maryland, but railroads were an even more stunning development. In 1830, the steam-driven locomotives of the Baltimore and Ohio (B & O) Railroad began providing the nation's first rail passenger service. The trains sped people and freight across the state at a then-dizzying 20 miles (32 kilometers) per hour. One Baltimore newspaper marveled, "Thus will scientific power conquer space, and even the Alleghenies sink . . . beneath the pressure of unconquered steam; nay, the laws of gravity give way before the march of mind."

Speed was the essence of the sleek clipper ships that swept in and out of Baltimore Harbor during the 1840s and 1850s. The clippers were descendants of the privateers that had earlier bedeviled British warships. They carried eager gold-seekers around Cape Horn on their way to California and traded with Africa, South America, and China.

THE SEEDS OF DISSENSION

Many of the workers on Maryland's canals and railroads were impoverished Irish Catholics who had come to the United States in search of a better life. A wave of German immigrants also surged into the Old Line State in the 1840s. Some longtime Marylanders, feeling that their jobs and even their way of life were threatened by the newcomers, rallied behind an antiforeign political party that sprang up in New York and Philadelphia. The party made its plans in secret, and when its members were questioned, they would reply that they knew nothing. For this reason, they were nicknamed the "Know-Nothings."

Through a variety of corrupt practices, the Know-Nothings

controlled elections in Maryland in the 1850s. One of their most scandalous methods of securing votes was known as "cooping." They rounded up destitute men and herded them into small rooms or pens, where they gave them whiskey or drugs. Then they led their "supporters" from one polling place to another and had them vote again and again.

To many white Marylanders, free blacks seemed even more threatening than foreigners. Many of these blacks had been given their freedom by their masters; others were the children of free parents. By the 1850s, more free blacks lived in Maryland than in any other state. White workers resented them because they competed for jobs. Also, many whites feared that the free blacks would stir rebellion among the state's slaves.

Slavery had never gained a foothold in western Maryland, and most Piedmont farmers disapproved of the institution. The tobacco planters of the Tidewater region, however, still depended heavily upon slaves to tend their crops. In 1824, Marylander Benjamin Lundy began to call for the gradual freeing of all slaves in his Baltimore newspaper *The Genius of Universal Emancipation*. Lundy was joined in 1828 by William Lloyd Garrison of Boston, who believed passionately that slavery must be abolished at once. "Slavery is a monster," Garrison wrote, "and must be treated as such—hunted down bravely and dispatched at a blow."

In general, slaves in Maryland were treated less harshly than those in the states farther south. Under Maryland law, a master was required to feed, clothe, and shelter slaves adequately, and was forbidden to give more than ten lashes with a whip as punishment. However, these laws were only loosely enforced.

In the northern states, the movement for the abolition of slavery gained more and more followers among whites and free blacks. Many slaves from Maryland escaped to freedom on the

Maryland-born former slave Harriet Tubman (far left, holding pan) helped hundreds of slaves—including the people in this photograph—escape to freedom along the Underground Railroad.

Underground Railroad, a secret system of "stations," or safe houses, where runaway slaves could find shelter. Free blacks or sympathetic whites (many of whom were Quakers) escorted runaways from one station to the next, often hiding them in wagons under loads of hay or corn.

One of the most famous "conductors" on the Underground Railroad was Harriet Tubman, who was born into slavery on a plantation in Dorchester County on the Eastern Shore. When she was sixteen, her master beat her so severely on the head with a brass paperweight that for the rest of her life she had frequent epileptic seizures. After she escaped to the North, Tubman vowed to lead others out of slavery as well. She made more than twenty perilous trips back into Maryland and led some three hundred slaves safely to freedom.

The majority of white Marylanders had never owned slaves, and many abhorred the slavery system. Yet most Marylanders resented being told what to do by outsiders. Maryland was strongly committed to the principle of states' rights—the right of each state to control its internal affairs.

In 1860, the antislavery Republican party nominated Abraham Lincoln to run for president. Many Marylanders feared that Lincoln would demand the immediate abolition of slavery if he became president. Maryland gave the majority of its popular votes to the proslavery candidate, John Breckinridge.

When news of Lincoln's victory reached the southern states, fear and anger boiled into a movement for secession. South Carolina led the way. By the spring of 1861, one southern state after another had broken away from the United States to form a new nation, the Confederate States of America. In the turbulent months after the election of 1860, Marylanders were torn between their sympathy for their southern neighbors and their loyalty to the Union.

THE BLUE AND THE GRAY

In southern Maryland and on the Eastern Shore, the tobacco planters were eager to join forces with the slaveholding Confederacy. But Unionist feeling was strong among the farmers of western Maryland, who had never owned slaves. The planters urged Governor Thomas Hicks to hold a special session of the legislature to consider secession. But Hicks stood firm, declaring, "Maryland should not seem to give continence to [disunion] by convening her legislature at the bidding of South Carolina."

The Civil War began on April 12, 1861, when Confederate troops attacked Fort Sumter in Charleston, South Carolina. In response, President Lincoln issued a call for troops to put down the rebellion in the South and reunite the Union. On April 19, one thousand Union troops, on their way from Massachusetts to Washington, D.C., arrived in Baltimore, where they had to change trains. As they crossed the city on their way to the B & O station, an angry mob followed them, shouting insults and pelting them with stones. When the mob began to hurl heavy cobblestones from the streets, the troops turned and opened fire. By the time the riot was over, four soldiers and twelve Baltimore citizens lay dead, and many other people were wounded. The blood shed in Baltimore was the first to be spilled in the long and disastrous Civil War.

Louisiana schoolteacher James Ryder Randall, a Marylander by birth, wrote a passionate song inspired by the Baltimore riot. It quickly became a marching song for the Confederacy, and today is Maryland's official state song. Its fiery words urged Marylanders to drive out the northern invaders:

> The despot's heel is on thy shore,
> Maryland, my Maryland!
> His torch is at thy temple door,
> Maryland, my Maryland!
> Avenge the patriotic gore
> That flecked the streets of Baltimore,
> And be the battle-queen of yore,
> Maryland, my Maryland!

If Maryland joined the Confederacy, the federal capital at Washington would be wholly surrounded by enemy territory. Unwilling to run such a risk, President Lincoln decided to keep Maryland in the Union by force. Throughout the war, Maryland was occupied by blue-uniformed Union troops who tried to stamp out all Confederate sentiment. They forbade the display of the Confederate flag or the playing of Confederate songs. Many prominent Marylanders, including twenty-six legislators, were imprisoned at Fort McHenry on suspicion that they had secessionist leanings.

During the course of the war, about twenty thousand

The 1862 Battle of Antietam was the bloodiest single day of fighting in American history.

Marylanders made their way south and put on gray Confederate uniforms. Thousands more became dedicated Union soldiers. Divided loyalties tore some families apart. In 1862, Confederate Major William Goldsborough of the Maryland Infantry captured his own brother, a surgeon with the Union army. As writer Lizette Reese later recalled, "Between the blue forces and the gray we were ground between two millstones of terror."

Late in the summer of 1862, Confederate troops under General Robert E. Lee launched a bold assault on Union territory. On September 17, forty-one thousand Confederate soldiers clashed with eighty-seven thousand Union troops at Antietam Creek near the town of Sharpsburg. The battle proved to be the bloodiest single day of fighting in American history.

The funeral train of President Abraham Lincoln

"At first [the cannonfire] sounded like pattering drops upon a roof," one newspaper reporter wrote later. "Then [it was] a roll, a crash, roar and rush, like a mighty ocean billow upon the shore . . . with deep and heavy explosions of the batteries like the crashing of thunderbolts." Both sides suffered horrifying casualties in the battle. Finally, the Confederate forces retreated across the Potomac.

When the smoke cleared, trees lay splintered, the earth was furrowed by artillery shells, and houses and barns were in ashes. Some twelve thousand Union men and eleven thousand Confederates had been killed or wounded. In a tent in the midst of this devastation, a young nurse named Clara Barton tended hundreds of wounded men with the primitive medicines available to her. At Hagerstown, Williamsport, and Frederick, churches and schools served as makeshift hospitals. Sharpsburg families cared for injured men in their homes and barns.

In the later years of the war, Confederate raiding parties tried to disrupt transportation in Maryland. They tore up railroad tracks, destroyed bridges, and dynamited locks of the Chesapeake and Ohio Canal. In the summer of 1864, Confederate troops threatened to burn Hagerstown and Frederick unless they were paid a heavy ransom in money and supplies. Both towns paid the ransom, but the invaders nevertheless looted many homes and shops. Confederate forces under General Jubal Early marched on Washington, D.C., but were driven back just outside the city.

On April 9, 1865, Robert E. Lee surrendered at Appomattox Court House, Virginia. Church bells rang and banners rippled in the breeze as the war-weary people of Maryland celebrated the end of this terrible conflict that had taken so many lives. But only five days later, word swept through the state and the nation that President Lincoln was dead, assassinated while attending a play in Washington, D.C.

Lincoln's assassin was an actor from Maryland named John Wilkes Booth. Fleeing the scene of the crime, he escaped into his home state before he was finally captured. In one official bulletin, Secretary of War Edwin Stanton accused the people of Prince Georges, Charles, and St. Marys counties of sheltering the fugitive out of hostility to the federal government.

Despite such accusations, however, most Marylanders were overwhelmed with grief in the days after Lincoln's death. On its long journey to Springfield, Illinois, the funeral train passed through Baltimore, and Lincoln's body lay in state for two hours in the rotunda of the Exchange Building. Thousands of mourners filed past the coffin to pay their last respects to the man who had fought so hard to save the Union.

Chapter 6

MARYLAND COMES OF AGE

SHUCKING DEPT.
W. H. KILLIAN CO.
BALTO., MD.

HUGHES CO.
BALTO.

MARYLAND COMES OF AGE

In 1867, delegates from all over Maryland met in Annapolis to write a new state constitution. The delegates hoped to draw on the lessons of Maryland's past while creating a code of laws that would serve their rapidly changing state. Yet even the most imaginative delegate at the convention could not have foreseen the changes that would sweep Maryland into the twentieth century.

THE STRUGGLE FOR CHANGE

Maryland abolished slavery in 1864, and a federal civil-rights act two years later eliminated many laws that had oppressed free blacks. In the years after the Civil War, black people in Maryland feverishly pursued education as a means of improving their lives. The federal Freedmen's Bureau and many charitable societies organized classes for adults who wanted to learn to read and write. Schools for black children opened in Baltimore and on the Eastern Shore.

Although slavery no longer existed, the separation of the races remained a deeply entrenched custom in Maryland. As early as 1872, a state law mandated "separate but equal" schools for blacks. Blacks had to use separate washrooms and drinking fountains and ride in separate railroad cars. Furthermore, regardless of their skills, black people were barred from entering many trades and professions.

In the late 1800s, Baltimore became a major manufacturing and food-processing center. Thousands of people sought work in the city's factories, where they made furniture, glass, paint, and textiles. Canning developed into one of the city's leading industries. Baltimore also became the nation's chief producer of pianos, with some fifteen piano-building firms.

Between 1870 and 1900, Baltimore's population nearly doubled. Most of the newcomers came from rural parts of Maryland, but many were immigrants from Germany, Great Britain, Ireland, Russia, Poland, and other European nations. Eager to start a better life, they often found little but dire poverty. They lived in small, overcrowded apartments, many of which lacked adequate running water. As was true in many of the nation's cities at this time, men, women, and even small children worked ten to twelve hours a day for pitifully low wages. One government report on Baltimore canneries describes "children, three years old and upward, training their fingers to the labor which is their share of the family toil."

Alarmed by these conditions, a group of Baltimore civic leaders founded the Charity Organization Society in 1881. The society raised money for scholarships, opened neighborhood houses that offered classes and recreation, and fought to eliminate child labor.

Three outstanding Baltimore businessmen—George Peabody, Johns Hopkins, and Enoch Pratt—made enduring contributions to their city's cultural life. In the 1850s, banker George Peabody began to plan a magnificent cultural institute that would include a library, conservatory of music, and art museum. The project—the Peabody Institute—was finally completed when the gallery of art opened in 1881. Johns Hopkins, a director of the Baltimore and Ohio Railroad, bequeathed $7 million for the establishment of the Johns Hopkins University for the Promotion of Education in Maryland. He also founded the Johns Hopkins Hospital and its

In the late 1800s, enduring contributions were made to Baltimore's cultural life by Johns Hopkins (top), who endowed Johns Hopkins University and Johns Hopkins Hospital; and George Peabody (bottom), who founded the Peabody Institute. The ornate Peabody Library (left) is today part of Johns Hopkins University.

affiliated school of medicine. Eccentric industrialist Enoch Pratt endowed his Free Library of Baltimore with a gift of precisely $833,333.33.

OYSTER WARS AND RAILROAD STRIKES

During the 1800s, Americans developed a ravenous appetite for Chesapeake Bay oysters. With the development of commercial canning in Baltimore in the 1820s, the highly perishable oysters could, for the first time, be preserved for shipment. For generations, oystermen in log canoes had gathered the shellfish from the bottom of the bay with long, scissorlike tongs. An 1865 law permitted Marylanders to harvest oysters by scouring the bottom with weighted nets or dredges. Dredging was much less tiring work than tonging, and a dredger could gather as many oysters in five minutes as a diligent tonger could collect in an hour.

In the late 1800s, in what became known as the "Oyster Wars," Maryland oystermen patrolled their portion of the bay to keep out "pirate dredgers" from Virginia.

In the decades that followed, the town of Crisfield on the Eastern Shore became the hub of Maryland's booming oyster trade. Thousands of men, women, and children worked in packinghouses, shucking oysters and loading them into barrels of ice. Crisfield took on the colorful atmosphere of a mining town in the Wild West, with noisy saloons, passionate poker games, and an occasional shoot-out.

Not surprisingly, outsiders were eager to break into Maryland's lucrative oyster business. From the 1870s through the early 1890s, "pirate dredgers" from Virginia slipped into Maryland waters. Maryland responded by creating an "oyster navy," consisting of several armed sloops, to patrol its portion of the bay. The "Oyster Wars" earned newspaper headlines across the nation and claimed several dozen lives.

Trouble of a different kind brewed among Maryland's railroad workers. In 1877, four leading companies, including the B & O,

Federal troops were called in to break up the 1877 Baltimore and Ohio railroad strike.

agreed to end a vicious rate war and to cut costs by slashing workers' wages. On July 16, B & O firemen walked off the job at Camden Junction just outside Baltimore. They were soon followed by the B & O engineers. The strike swept across the state to West Virginia and Pittsburgh, Pennsylvania. During the long week that followed, railroad workers looted boxcars, and ten people died when riots broke out in Cumberland. When fifteen thousand strikers gathered in Baltimore's Camden Square, Governor John Lee Carroll asked the president of the United States to send in federal troops.

The army finally broke the railroad strike of 1877, but eventually Maryland adopted strong legislation to protect the rights of laborers. In 1902, Maryland became the first state in the nation to pass a law providing for the compensation of workers injured on the job.

WARTIME AND PEACETIME

In 1917, the United States entered the great war that was sweeping across Europe. During World War I, thousands of workers took jobs in Maryland's war plants. Shipyards at Baltimore and Sparrows Point turned out naval vessels. The value of the state's canning industry increased 58 percent, and agricultural output more than doubled as Maryland rushed to meet the needs of a hungry army.

In 1918, Maryland congressmen ratified the Eighteenth Amendment to the Constitution, prohibiting the manufacture and sale of alcoholic beverages throughout the nation. Almost at once, however, Marylanders began to defy the new law. In 1922, Governor Albert C. Ritchie declared that Marylanders considered Prohibition to be "an unnecessary and drastic federal infringement upon state and personal rights." Baltimore journalist H. L. Mencken wrote that "such laws deserve no respect, and deserving no respect they deserve no obedience." Maryland's resistance to Prohibition gave rise to one of its nicknames, the "Free State"—free from outside interference.

The nation's economy boomed throughout the 1920s, but the 1930s ushered in the worst depression in the country's history. By 1932, six out of ten factories in Maryland had closed or cut production. In Baltimore, families stood in line to receive day-old loaves of bread. On the Eastern Shore, people tried to survive by fishing and gathering wild herbs.

Governor Ritchie, who held office for an unprecedented fourteen years, raised money for unemployment relief by radically cutting other expenditures in the state budget. Further help came through the "New Deal" programs of President Franklin D. Roosevelt. About $160 million was channeled into Maryland

under the New Deal, including some $40 million in direct
assistance to jobless workers and their families. Federal programs
created jobs refurbishing the old Chesapeake and Delaware Canal
and building a new Hall of Records in Annapolis. The Civilian
Conservation Corps (CCC) employed thousands of young men to
plant trees, control erosion, and develop outdoor recreation areas.

When the United States entered World War II in 1941,
Maryland's factories suddenly hummed again. In proportion to
population, Maryland ranked fourth among the states in federal
military contracts. At its Sparrows Point plant and Fairfield
Shipyard, the Bethlehem Steel Company made everything from
nails to Liberty ships. Fairchild Aircraft of Hagerstown assembled
bombers and cargo planes. Farm prices rose once more, with yet
another hungry army to feed.

Throughout the war, Maryland buzzed with military activity.
Some 3.5 million servicemen and servicewomen underwent basic
training at Fort Meade in Anne Arundel County. In 1942,
Andrews Air Force Base opened for the defense of Washington,
D.C. The earth shook at the Aberdeen Proving Ground as military
engineers tested ammunition, weapons, and tanks. In Edgewood,
the Army Chemical Center developed flamethrowers and

Gas mortars were developed at the Army Chemical Center in Edgewood during World War II.

incendiary bombs, while experiments in biological warfare were carried out at Camp Detrick near Frederick.

Twice during the summer of 1942, German submarines briefly blockaded Chesapeake Bay, bringing the war frighteningly close to home for the people of Maryland. During the course of the war, young men from the Old Line State fought courageously in the Maryland 29th Infantry Division, nicknamed the "Blue and Gray." The 29th served with distinction during the decisive Battle of Normandy in 1944.

CHALLENGING THE OLD WAYS

In 1935, a black student named Donald Murray was refused admission to the University of Maryland School of Law, solely because of his race. In the 1930s, such instances of discrimination were not uncommon. This time, however, the student took his case to court. With the help of a brilliant young lawyer named Thurgood Marshall, Murray became the first black student to enter a professional school at a state university south of Mason and Dixon's Line. In a dawning civil-rights movement, black

In the 1960s, blacks in Maryland fought racial discrimination with such techniques as the sit-in. This man was dragged away by police after refusing to leave a segregated lunch counter in Cambridge, Maryland, in 1963.

people in Maryland and throughout the nation had begun to fight for equal treatment under the laws of the land.

During the 1950s and 1960s, blacks in Maryland were able to participate in state and local government for the first time. In 1954, the first blacks were elected to the state legislature. By 1973, the legislature included eighteen black members. In Baltimore, blacks "sat in" at lunch counters and theaters until the "Whites Only" signs disappeared. In 1967, Maryland repealed a three-hundred-year-old law banning marriages between blacks and whites, and became the first state south of Mason and Dixon's Line to adopt a law against racial discrimination in new housing.

In the decades after World War II, Maryland followed the nationwide trend toward suburbanization. Families who could afford to buy new homes left the cities for the green grass and clean air of the suburbs. Most of the new suburbanites were affluent and white, while those who remained in the cities tended to be poor and black. Between 1952 and 1972, Baltimore's white population declined by 50 percent. As the city's tax base crumbled, schools and other public facilities began to deteriorate. At the same time, jobs grew more scarce as many factories cut back

Harborplace, a shopping complex that opened in 1980, was part of a vast urban-renewal project undertaken in Baltimore in the 1980s.

production. In 1968, following the assassination of Dr. Martin Luther King, Jr., the frustrations of Baltimore's blacks exploded in a series of street riots that destroyed millions of dollars' worth of property and left some city blocks in charred ruins.

In an effort to revive Baltimore's economy, a group of businessmen raised funds to develop Charles Center, a complex of high-rise apartments, shopping plazas, and theaters in the downtown business district. The success of Charles Center led to the renovation of decaying waterfront property along Baltimore's Inner Harbor. In 1980, the twin glass pavilions of Harborplace, a beautiful arcade of shops and restaurants, opened to the public. The Inner Harbor project also included the National Aquarium, a thirty-story World Trade Center, and a marina.

Baltimore was the first major American city to undertake such an immense renovation. Its renewal projects enhanced downtown Baltimore and channeled money back into the city. Yet thousands of families still lived in poverty. According to one Baltimore judge, "This great city has built marvelous buildings . . . which have created a spirit of hope for the rejuvenation of Baltimore. But all around these beautiful buildings . . . are large numbers of children with dashed hopes of decent education, broken families with unemployable parents, hundreds of thousands of functionally illiterate people of all ages, races, and creeds. . . . We must continue to build great buildings, but we must concentrate more than ever before on building great people."

In 1966, a daring real-estate developer named James Rouse broke ground for a new model city in the heart of Howard County, between Baltimore and Washington, D.C. Rouse hoped to create an ideal community where people could live and work together comfortably despite their differences. As he recruited residents for his city, which he named Columbia, he sought to maintain a racial and religious balance. To ensure a sense of community among the residents, he divided Columbia into nine "villages." Each village contained three or four "neighborhoods" built around central schools and playgrounds.

By the late 1980s, Columbia was a thriving small city. Yet some residents felt disillusioned. Columbia had many of the same problems as other towns. There were not enough jobs within the city, nor did it provide enough housing for people with low incomes. Rouse's bold experiment succeeded in many ways, but it did not produce a perfect community.

Three and a half centuries before, Cecil Calvert had also dreamed of creating an ideal community on Maryland soil. Yet no one on earth has ever found a way for people to live together in complete harmony. Though Maryland has never been a utopia, its remarkable diversity has created a unique sense of tolerance among its people. Their past triumphs over adversity equip Marylanders to face with confidence the challenges of the future.

Chapter 7

GOVERNMENT AND THE ECONOMY

GOVERNMENT AND THE ECONOMY

GOVERNMENT

Maryland's present state constitution, which has been amended many times, was ratified in 1867. Under the constitution, the state government is divided into three main branches. The legislative branch makes and repeals laws. The judicial branch interprets the laws, and the executive branch ensures that the laws are enforced.

The Maryland legislature, or General Assembly, meets annually at the State House in Annapolis on the second Wednesday in January for a ninety-day session. The General Assembly consists of two houses. The upper house, or senate, has 47 members; 141 members serve in the lower house, or house of representatives. All state legislators are elected to four-year terms.

On the local level, Maryland's judicial system consists of twelve district courts. The state also has eight circuit courts. From the circuit courts, cases may be appealed to the court of special appeals. The highest court in the state is the court of appeals, composed of seven judges. The governor appoints judges to the courts of appeals, but the judges must be approved by the voters at the next general election following their appointment.

Elected officials in the executive branch of the government include the governor, lieutenant governor, attorney general, and comptroller. The governor may not serve more than two consecutive terms in office. The governor appoints a secretary of state, adjutant general, and members of various state boards, including the board of education.

Left: A chapel at the University of Maryland at College Park
Right: Midshipmen at the United States Naval Academy in Annapolis

EDUCATION

The first publicly funded school in the Maryland Colony, King William's School, opened in 1696. In 1826, Maryland's legislature provided for the establishment of public schools throughout the state. Today, all Maryland children between the ages of six and fifteen are required to attend school.

Maryland is noted for its many outstanding schools of higher learning. Founded in 1876, Johns Hopkins University in Baltimore is world renowned for its schools of medicine, public health, and international studies. St. John's College in Annapolis offers a unique undergraduate program based on the study of one hundred "Great Books of Western Civilization." Other privately funded colleges in the state include Goucher College, in Towson; Hood College, in Frederick; Washington College, in Chestertown; and Western Maryland College, in Westminster.

Cargo containers at the Port of Baltimore

The main campus of the University of Maryland is located in College Park. Among Maryland's many other state colleges and universities are Bowie State University, in Bowie; Frostburg State University, in Frostburg; Morgan State University, in Baltimore; Salisbury State University, in Salisbury; and Towson State University, in Baltimore.

Since 1845, Annapolis has been the home of the United States Naval Academy. Every Wednesday afternoon in spring and fall, columns of midshipmen (as undergraduates are called) in full-dress uniform maneuver on the parade ground. The Naval Academy's Bancroft Hall, threaded with 5 miles (8 kilometers) of corridors and housing four thousand students, is the largest dormitory in the world.

TRANSPORTATION

Baltimore is one of the busiest ports on the Atlantic coast. Ships from Baltimore's docks reach the open sea by way of Chesapeake Bay, or by passing through the Chesapeake and Delaware Canal into Delaware Bay. The Chesapeake and Delaware Canal handles

Near Annapolis, the Eastern Shore and the Western Shore are linked by
the twin spans of the Chesapeake Bay Bridge.

more traffic each year than does the Panama Canal. Cambridge,
Maryland's second-largest port city, is a major center for the
shipping of seafood.

Opened in 1952, the Chesapeake Bay Bridge links the Eastern
Shore with the rest of Maryland. Arching 4.5 miles (7 kilometers)
across the bay from Kent Island to Annapolis, the bridge proved
so popular that a second, parallel span was opened in 1980.
Several bridges cross the Potomac, including the Woodrow Wilson
Bridge just below Washington, D.C.

Maryland has about 135 airports. The largest and busiest of
these is Baltimore-Washington International Airport (BWI) in
Friendship, just south of Baltimore. Cars and trucks speed across
Maryland over some 27,400 miles (44,095 kilometers) of paved
roads and highways. About 1,000 miles (1,609 kilometers) of
railroad track crisscross the state, and both freight and passenger
trains serve Baltimore.

Beef cattle grazing on a Maryland pasture

COMMUNICATION

Maryland's first newspaper, the *Maryland Gazette*, appeared weekly in Annapolis between 1727 and 1734. Today Maryland has about eighty newspapers, fifteen of them published daily. The largest daily newspaper in the state is Baltimore's *Sun*, which has won several Pulitzer prizes for fine reporting.

Radio came to Maryland in 1922, when WCAO and WFBR went on the air in Baltimore. The state's first television station, WMAR-TV, began broadcasting in Baltimore in 1947. Today Maryland has 105 AM and FM radio stations and 15 television stations.

AGRICULTURE

Agriculture accounts for about 1 percent of Maryland's gross state product, or GSP—the total value of goods and services produced annually within the state. Nearly 45 percent of Maryland's land is devoted to farming.

Livestock production makes up about two-thirds of Maryland's agricultural output. Maryland is a leading producer of broilers (chickens between five and twelve weeks of age). Most broilers are raised around Salisbury on the Eastern Shore. Dairy cattle graze on the hillsides of Frederick County. Maryland also produces beef cattle, eggs, and hogs.

During colonial days, tobacco was the backbone of Maryland's economy. Today it is third among the state's cash crops, outranked by corn and soybeans. Maryland growers also produce apples, strawberries, cucumbers, hay, snap beans, tomatoes, and wheat. Maryland greenhouses and nurseries raise ornamental trees and shrubs.

NATURAL RESOURCES

Nature endowed Maryland with a wealth of mineral reserves. Crushed stone, valuable in the construction industry, is quarried in the state's Piedmont region. Quarries at Cockeysville furnished marble for the Washington Monument in the nation's capital. Soft, or bituminous, coal is mined in Garrett and Allegany counties, especially in the Georges Creek Valley. Garrett County has deposits of natural gas.

Fisheries are another vital natural resource in Maryland. Off the Atlantic coast, fishermen catch flounder and tuna. Chesapeake Bay yields bluefish, catfish, striped bass, bullheads, white perch, eels, soft-shell crabs, and menhaden, and is famous for its clams and oysters. By the late nineteenth century, oysters had become an immensely popular delicacy. Since the 1890s, oysters have been cultivated in man-made beds.

The Eastern
Shore is a
leading producer
of broilers
(top right),
while Chesapeake
Bay is famous
for its clams,
oysters, crabs
(top left,
bottom), and
other kinds of
seafood.

Food processing is Maryland's second-largest industry.

MANUFACTURING

Manufacturing accounts for about 14 percent of Maryland's GSP. Electrical machinery, including computers and other high-tech equipment, is among the state's leading manufactured products. Plants in and around Baltimore prepare processed meats, frozen foods, and dried spices, and Cambridge is a major center for seafood packaging.

The chemical industry is another essential ingredient in Maryland's economy. Baltimore factories produce such household items as paints and soap. Other firms in the state manufacture drugs, cosmetics, and fertilizers.

SERVICE INDUSTRIES

After World War II, Maryland's economy shifted away from manufacturing and came to depend more and more heavily upon service industries. Rather than producing salable goods, service industries offer services to groups or individuals. These services

The NASA/Goddard Space Flight Center in Greenbelt

include health care, education, advertising, and data processing. Retail salespeople, beauticians, bus drivers, telephone operators, hotel managers, attorneys, physicians, and real-estate brokers are all part of the service economy. Today, service industries comprise about 80 percent of Maryland's GSP.

The largest single employer in Maryland's service industries is the federal government. Many Marylanders work on military bases, such as Fort Meade, Andrews Air Force Base, and the Patuxent Naval Air Station in St. Marys County. In addition to military facilities, Maryland is home to many federal agencies, including the National Institutes of Health in Bethesda, the Federal Census Bureau in Suitland, the National Aeronautics and Space Administration (NASA) in Greenbelt, the National Bureau of Standards in Gaithersburg, and the Social Security Administration in Baltimore.

Chapter 8

ARTS AND RECREATION

ARTS AND RECREATION

Maryland writers have portrayed the most horrifying and the most comic aspects of human existence. The state's artists have captured the warmth and detail of everyday scenes and the magnificence of mythic heroes. Athletes from the Old Line State are counted among the world's champions. Maryland's richly varied cultural heritage is a reflection of the state's remarkable diversity.

LITERATURE

Father Andrew White, a Jesuit priest who arrived at St. Clements Island with Lord Baltimore's first colonists, created the earliest written account of life in Maryland. His *Relatio Itineris in Marylandium*, written in Latin, was published in 1635. A rather glorified picture of colonial life emerges in *A Character of the Province of Maryland*, written by George Alsop in 1666. Some historians believe that Alsop came to Maryland as an indentured servant.

A more humorous version of life in the colony appears in *The Sot-Weed Factor*, a long satirical poem by Ebenezer Cooke. Published in London in 1708, the poem depicts the misfortunes of an English tobacco merchant, or "factor," who ventures into Maryland.

The first Maryland writer to earn national acclaim was a clergyman named Mason Locke Weems. His biography *The Life and Memorable Activities of George Washington* is the source of the legend of Washington's boyhood mishap with the hatchet and the cherry tree.

Between 1792 and 1802, a free black man from Maryland named Benjamin Banneker published the *Pennsylvania, Delaware, Maryland, and Virginia Almanac and Ephemeris.* Banneker was a self-taught mathematician and astronomer, and his almanac was crammed with information about the stars and planets. He also helped survey the District of Columbia and wrote numerous essays protesting slavery and pointing out the folly of war.

The Delphian Society was a group of poets, novelists, and critics that flourished in Baltimore in the early 1800s. The society's most prominent member was John Neal, who edited a literary magazine called *The Portico.* Few people read Neal's fiction today, but he is still remembered as the first critic to praise the work of a young writer named Edgar Allan Poe.

Born in Boston, Massachusetts, Poe lived in Baltimore from 1831 to 1834. During this time, he published the first of many short stories dealing with the macabre and the supernatural. Among Poe's works are such chilling tales as "The Tell-Tale Heart," "The Black Cat," and "The Fall of the House of Usher." His poem "The Raven" contains the sinister refrain, "Quoth the raven, 'Nevermore!' " Poe's "The Murders in the Rue Morgue" is considered to be the first modern detective story.

Poe returned to Baltimore in 1849. According to some accounts, he was a victim of the practice of "cooping"—being forced to vote again and again while being kept in a drunken stupor. Already in poor health, Poe died in Baltimore and was buried in Westminster Churchyard.

In the 1830s, Edgar Allan Poe (above) lived in this house in Baltimore (left).

A vivid narrative of life under slavery is the autobiography of Frederick Douglass, *My Bondage and My Freedom*, first published in 1845 and revised several times. Douglass was born a slave in Talbot County on the Eastern Shore. He worked as a field hand on a tobacco plantation and as a ship caulker in Baltimore before he escaped to the North at the age of twenty-one. In Massachusetts, he became an eloquent spokesman for the abolitionist cause. After the Civil War, Douglass continued to work for the rights of black people. He also championed the cause of women's rights.

Social criticism of a different kind flowed from the satirical pen of Henry Louis (H. L.) Mencken, a regular columnist with the Baltimore *Sun*. During the 1920s and 1930s, Mencken humorously criticized middle-class American life, big business, and organized religion. In one essay, he declared, "Conscience is the inner voice that warns us somebody may be looking."

A satirist with a lighter touch was Ogden Nash, who spent most of his later life in Baltimore. Nash published twenty volumes of humorous verse, including such engaging titles as *I'm a Stranger Here Myself* and *Everyone but Thee and Me*. Typical of Nash's verse is this short poem, which parodies Joyce Kilmer's famous poem "Trees" as it comments on the view along America's highways:

> I think that I shall never see
> A billboard lovely as a tree.
> Indeed, unless the billboard fall
> I'll never see a tree at all.

Two highly acclaimed contemporary novelists from Maryland are John Barth and Anne Tyler. John Barth was born in Cambridge, and many of his novels are set on the Eastern Shore. His works, such as *The Floating Opera* and *Giles Goat-Boy*, are densely philosophical novels that experiment with new literary techniques. *The Sot-Weed Factor* (a title he borrowed from Ebenezer Cooke) parodies eighteenth-century English fiction. Anne Tyler began living in Baltimore in the late 1960s. Baltimore is the backdrop for several of her novels, including *Searching for Caleb, Dinner at the Homesick Restaurant,* and *The Accidental Tourist.* Tyler won the 1989 Pulitzer Prize in fiction for her novel *Breathing Lessons.*

ART

During the eighteenth century, Annapolis was the hub of culture in Maryland. Among the artists drawn to the city was German-born portrait painter Justus Engelhart Kuhn, who worked there from 1708 to 1717. Kuhn's many fine portraits of children are rich with the details of everyday colonial life. One of his paintings contains the first depiction in American art of a black slave.

Born in Queen Annes County in 1741, Charles Willson Peale learned the saddler's trade as a young man. His artistic career

Maryland-born artist Charles Willson Peale painted portraits of many famous Americans of his day, including Supreme Court Justice Samuel Chase (left), also a Marylander.

began when he traded a saddle for a few painting lessons from a famous German artist. In 1766, a group of Maryland painters arranged to send Peale to London, where he continued his studies for three years. In 1775, he set up a studio in Philadelphia, where he spent the rest of his life. Peale painted many of the great leaders of his time, including George Washington, John Adams, Thomas Jefferson, and Benjamin Franklin. He was also fascinated by science. One of his paintings records his discovery of a mastodon skeleton on a farm in New York.

Peale believed that, with proper instruction, almost anyone could learn to paint well. He taught his brother James and his sons Raphael and Rembrandt to paint, and all of them became respected artists. Rembrandt Peale is remembered in Maryland as the founder of the state's first museum of art. Founded in 1814 as

Baltimore's Washington Monument, unveiled in 1829, was the first major monument erected to George Washington.

the Baltimore Museum and Gallery of Fine Arts, it is today known as the Peale Museum.

Baltimore was the first American city to commission impressive historical monuments, earning it the nickname "the Monumental City." In 1829, Baltimoreans cheered at the unveiling of their Washington Monument. Its 164-foot (50-meter) column was designed by architect Robert Mills. The column is crowned by a 16-foot (5-meter) statue of the first president that was created by Italian-born sculptor Enrico Causici. The Battle Monument, designed by Maximilian Godefroy and commemorating Baltimore's role in the War of 1812, was completed a year later by another Italian sculptor who had settled in the city, Antonio Cappellano.

The works of nineteenth-century painter Frank D. Mayer reflect the artist's pride in Maryland history. Among Mayer's finest paintings are *The Burning of the Peggy Stewart* and *The Founding of*

Maryland, both of which today hang in the Maryland State House. Many of Mayer's paintings portray life in colonial Annapolis.

Sometimes called the "father of Maryland sculpture," Hans Schuler created many of the monuments that stand in Baltimore's Mount Vernon Place. Schuler had a powerful influence on art in Maryland during the late 1800s, when he was director of the Maryland Institute of Art in Baltimore. The Maryland Institute remains central to the artistic life of the state, attracting excellent students and instructors and bringing many outstanding exhibitions to Baltimore.

PERFORMING ARTS

Baltimore is the center of performing arts in Maryland today. The Lyric Theater is home to the Baltimore Symphony Orchestra and the Baltimore Opera. The Peabody Conservatory is among the nation's leading schools of music, and its students and faculty delight Baltimoreans with frequent performances.

Maryland playgoers flock to Baltimore's Morris A. Mechanic Theater and the Center Stage Repertory Theater. Baltimore's Theater Project brings experimental drama, avant-garde music, poetry readings, and mime shows to scattered locations throughout the city. The Maryland Hall for the Performing Arts in Annapolis is the home of the Annapolis Symphony Orchestra and Ballet Theatre of Annapolis.

SPORTS

Over the years, Baltimore's professional sports teams have produced magic moments in sports and many bigger-than-life superstars.

The Orioles (right) have fielded such fine players as Cal Ripken, Jr. (above).

For decades, legions of pro-football fans were devoted followers of the Baltimore Colts. The extent of fan loyalty in the city was illustrated by a character in the popular movie *Diner*, who refused to marry his fiancée until she passed a Colts trivia test. In the 1950s and 1960s, the Colts nurtured such football greats as Alan Ameche, Gene "Big Daddy" Lipscomb, Lenny Moore, and one of the finest quarterbacks of all time, Johnny Unitas. The 1958 championship game between the Colts and the New York Giants is considered by some to have been the most exciting professional football game ever played. But despite the popularity of the Colts, owner Robert Irsay moved the team to Indianapolis in 1984. Baltimore fans have never forgiven Irsay and the Colts management.

In baseball, the Baltimore Orioles have had no such unhappy endings. It is only fitting that the city where George Herman "Babe" Ruth was born should have a successful baseball team. In 1954, the St. Louis Browns moved to Baltimore, where they became the Orioles. In the early 1970s, under manager Earl Weaver, the Orioles assembled one of the great teams of modern times. Oriole stars of the 1960s and 1970s included Frank Robinson, Brooks Robinson, Paul Blair, and Jim Palmer. Cal Ripken, Jr., was an

Every year, Baltimore's Pimlico Race Track hosts the Preakness Stakes, part of horse racing's famous Triple Crown.

Oriole great of the 1980s. The Orioles thrilled all of Maryland by capturing World Series crowns in 1966, 1970, and 1983.

The rolling fields of central Maryland have long attracted horse lovers. The Maryland Jockey Club, founded in the 1700s, is the oldest racing association in America. The Maryland Hunt Cup Race is a popular cross-country steeplechase on a 4-mile (6.4-kilometer) course through the Worthington Valley. Every May, racing enthusiasts flock to Pimlico Race Track for the running of the Preakness, the second leg of horse racing's Triple Crown. The winning horse is draped with a blanket of black-eyed Susans, Maryland's state flower.

Maryland is one of the few states in the nation to claim a state sport, and it is an unusual one at that—the medieval contest of jousting. Since 1842, Marylanders have taken part in annual jousting tournaments. Skilled riders gallop down a field at full speed and try to spear dangling rings with a lance. Jousting is especially popular in southern Maryland, where tournaments are held in many communities from August to October.

Chapter 9

HIGHLIGHTS OF
THE OLD LINE STATE

HIGHLIGHTS OF THE OLD LINE STATE

In 1961, Maryland became the first state to establish a public agency for historic preservation. The Maryland Historical Trust awakened fresh interest in Maryland's heritage. Eagerly, many communities restored colonial homes, preserved Civil War battle sites, and celebrated their traditions of boat building, sailing, and oystering. At the same time, Maryland's cities and towns continued to grow, attracting new people and new industries.

Today the visitor can enjoy Maryland's stunning natural beauty and touch its deep historic roots. But there is another Maryland, a state that offers the fast pace of city life and all the wonders of high technology. In Maryland, the past and the future seem to stand shoulder to shoulder.

WESTERN MARYLAND

Western Maryland is a rugged strip of mountainous country scored by deep valleys and rushing streams. Every summer, white-water rafters tackle the Youghiogheny River (affectionately known as the "Yock") as it tumbles north into Pennsylvania. Naturalists may explore the unique Cranesville Sub-Arctic Swamp near Oakland, the habitat of many species of lichens and other plants ordinarily found near the Arctic Circle.

To the north, tucked between Garrett State Forest and Savage River State Forest, lies Deep Creek Lake. Originally created to

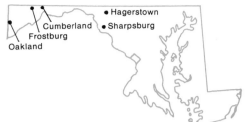

Great Falls Tavern is a famous landmark along the Chesapeake and Ohio Canal National Historical Park, which stretches from Cumberland to Washington, D.C.

provide hydroelectric power, Deep Creek Lake is a popular summer resort.

The town of Frostburg grew up around a tavern owned by a frontiersman named Meshach Frost. Today, many artifacts of the region's history are housed at the Frostburg Museum. Frostburg State University maintains three rooms of exhibits about coal mining in Maryland during the 1800s.

Just south of Cumberland, a replica of a mule-drawn canal boat floats on the old Chesapeake and Ohio Canal. Nearby, three lift locks are still in operation. As part of the Chesapeake and Ohio National Historical Park, ambitious hikers can follow the towpath along the C & O for 184.5 miles (297 kilometers), all the way from Cumberland to the Georgetown section of Washington, D.C.

A reenactment at Antietam National Battlefield

Hagerstown stands amid the farms and orchards of the broad
Hagerstown Valley, the most fertile section of western Maryland.
Near the center of town is the Jonathan Hager House, the 1739
home of the community's founder. The Hager House was built
over two natural springs that provided an abundant water supply
during Indian attacks. Today, the house is a museum devoted to
Maryland archaeology and frontier life.

History will forever remember Sharpsburg as the scene of the
Civil War's devastating Battle of Antietam. At the Antietam
National Battlefield, history buffs can follow the course of the
fighting around such landmarks as Burnside Bridge, the Dunker
Church, and Bloody Lane. Dedicated in 1865, the Antietam
National Cemetery contains the graves of more than five thousand
American soldiers who died in the Civil War and later conflicts.

CENTRAL MARYLAND

The Piedmont Plateau crosses central Maryland, a region of low, rolling hills. This part of the state is famous for its fine horses and cattle. The town of Frederick was the home of Francis Scott Key, composer of "The Star-Spangled Banner"; and of Roger Taney, chief justice of the United States Supreme Court during the mid-1800s. The lives of both men are celebrated at the Roger Brooke Taney and Francis Scott Key Museum, housed in Taney's reconstructed home.

Frederick is also known for the legend of Barbara Fritchie. At the age of ninety, it is said, Barbara Fritchie defied Confederate General Stonewall Jackson's order to lower the Union flag as he marched through the city in 1862. The incident is immortalized in the lines of John Greenleaf Whittier's poem "Barbara Fritchie":

> "Shoot if you must this old gray head,
> But spare your country's flag," she said.

No one knows if the story is true, but the home of the actual Barbara Fritchie has been carefully reconstructed and is open to the public.

On Catoctin Mountain, overlooking the town of Thurmont, stands Camp David, the official retreat of the president of the United States. Camp David was built by Franklin D. Roosevelt, who originally called it Shangri-La. President Dwight D. Eisenhower renamed it in honor of his grandson David. The world watched when American President Jimmy Carter, Israeli Prime Minister Menachem Begin, and Egyptian President Anwar el-Sadat met at Camp David for peace talks in 1978. This historic meeting led to the Camp David Accords, which ended a long conflict between Egypt and Israel.

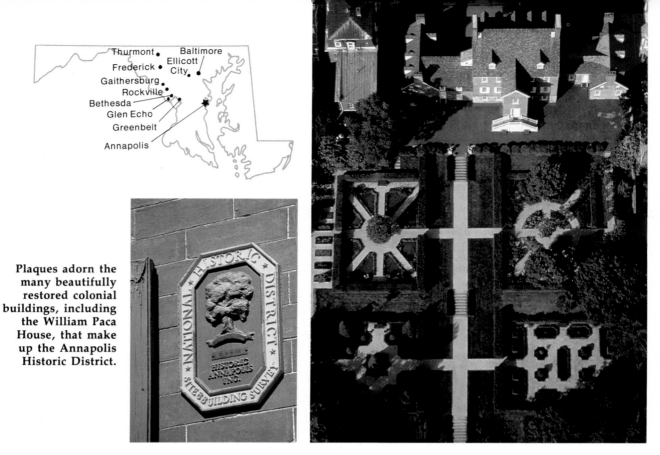

Thurmont •   Baltimore •
Frederick •   Ellicott
City •
Gaithersburg •
Rockville •
Bethesda •
Glen Echo •
Greenbelt •

Annapolis •

Plaques adorn the
many beautifully
restored colonial
buildings, including
the William Paca
House, that make
up the Annapolis
Historic District.

Ellicott City arose as a grain-milling town. Many of the town's original stone buildings have been carefully preserved, including several that once served as homes for mill workers. The B & O Railroad Station Museum recalls Ellicott City's role as an original passenger terminus on the B & O line. Today, the town's many shops are an antique-lover's delight.

Southwest of Ellicott City is Rockville, a thriving suburban center in the Washington metropolitan area. Along the tree-lined brick sidewalks of downtown Rockville's historic district stand more than one hundred stately nineteenth-century houses.

The achievements of Clara Barton are honored at her home in Glen Echo, now designated the Clara Barton National Historical Park. Barton's home once served as headquarters for the American Red Cross, the humanitarian organization she founded.

Many of the federal agencies located near Washington, D.C.,

offer fascinating guided tours. Engineers at the National Institute of Standards and Technology in Gaithersburg demonstrate methods for maintaining productivity and quality control. Visitors to the National Institutes of Health in Bethesda can tour a model research laboratory. The Goddard Space Flight Center at the National Aeronautics and Space Administration (NASA) in Greenbelt sponsors simulated rocket launches twice a month.

THE CAPITAL CITY

Maryland's capital, Annapolis, is a charming small city on Chesapeake Bay. The Maryland State House, begun in 1772, is the nation's oldest state capitol in continous use. Its octagonal wooden dome was built entirely without nails. The State House served as the nation's capitol from November 26, 1783, until August 13, 1784. The Old Senate Chamber of the State House was the site of two important historical events. On December 23, 1783, George Washington resigned as commander-in-chief of the Continental army in this room, and on January 14, 1784, the Treaty of Paris, ending the Revolutionary War, was ratified there.

Annapolis claims more eighteenth-century brick buildings than any other city in the nation. Many of these structures have been painstakingly restored in the Annapolis Historic District. The Hammond-Harwood House, built in 1774, is considered a masterpiece of Georgian design. The William Paca House is the restored home of one of Maryland's signers of the Declaration of Independence. Paca's terraced gardens were excavated from beneath a parking lot and have been enchantingly reconstructed. The gardens sprawl over 2 acres (.8 hectare) and include a domed pavilion, a Chinese trellised bridge, and a pond shaped like a fish. The restored Mt. Moriah Church, completed in 1876 by a black

The Maryland State House overlooking the Annapolis harbor

African Methodist Episcopal congregation, now houses the Banneker-Douglass Museum of Afro-American Life and History. The museum preserves artifacts of the lives of two of Maryland's leading black citizens, Benjamin Banneker and Frederick Douglass, and traces the history of African Americans in the state and the nation.

The broad Severn River harbor that blends into Chesapeake Bay is essential to the life of Annapolis. Hundreds of yachts berth at City Dock, and in October, Annapolis hosts some of the nation's biggest sailboat and powerboat shows. The bay provides a livelihood for many watermen, who set out with dredges or hydraulic tongs to harvest crabs and oysters. Annapolis, famous for its fine seafood, is sometimes referred to as "Crabtown."

The United States Naval Academy also depends on access to the bay. The stained glass windows of the magnificent Naval Academy Chapel commemorate many of the nation's naval heroes. The United States Naval Academy Museum displays uniforms,

weapons, maps, photographs, and one of the world's finest
collections of model ships.

THE CITY OF NEIGHBORHOODS

Every September, Baltimore hosts the annual City Fair, an
extravaganza of free concerts, games of chance, and more than one
hundred booths selling every imaginable ethnic dish, from Greek
grape leaves to Chinese egg rolls to Mexican tamales. Baltimore
has often been called the "City of Neighborhoods" because it is
made up of many different ethnic enclaves. Near the Inner Harbor
is a twelve-block area known as Little Italy. Poles and other
Eastern Europeans live in the Highlandtown section, Greeks in
"Greektown" further east, and Hispanics in Fells Point. Black
families live in West and Northwest Baltimore, while the city's
northwestern suburbs are predominantly Jewish. Blocks of row

Left: Baltimore's City Hall
Above: An example of the row houses with marble front steps for which Baltimore is famous

houses with white marble doorsteps are a signature of Baltimore's neighborhoods.

The statues of many American leaders adorn Baltimore's Mount Vernon Place. The oldest of these is the Washington Monument, designed by architect Robert Mills and crowned with a statue by Enrico Causici. Other statues on the square depict Justice Roger Brooke Taney and philanthropist George Peabody. Down the street stands the Maryland Historical Society and the adjoining Enoch Pratt House.

Among the treasures at the Maryland Historical Society is Francis Scott Key's original manuscript of "The Star-Spangled Banner." A replica of the flag that survived the Battle of Baltimore is on exhibit at the Star-Spangled Banner Flag House and 1812 War Museum. The original banner, which measured 30 feet by 40 feet (9 meters by 12 meters) and had 15 stars, was created by a Baltimore seamstress named Mary Pickersgill. Her life and times are documented as part of the museum's displays.

The cultural center of Maryland, Baltimore is home to several outstanding art galleries and museums. The Baltimore Museum of Art displays early Christian mosaics, Asian carvings, paintings from the Italian Renaissance, American crafts, and contemporary painting and sculpture. The Walters Art Gallery, donated to the city by Henry Walters in 1931, houses art objects spanning six thousand years. The Peale Museum, which opened in 1814, contains a fine collection of American paintings, including many by its founder, Rembrandt Peale. Natural-gas lighting was used for the first time in Baltimore when Peale installed gas lighting at the museum in 1816.

The house where Edgar Allan Poe lived from 1832 to 1835 has been carefully restored with furnishings of the period. Another Baltimore landmark is the nineteenth-century row house overlooking Union Square that was the home of journalist H. L. Mencken. Priceless original manuscripts and other documents pertaining to Poe and Mencken are gathered at the Enoch Pratt Free Library.

Each year, thousands of baseball fans pay homage to America's favorite pastime at the Babe Ruth Birthplace and Baltimore Orioles Museum. The second-largest baseball museum in the country, it preserves memorabilia of Ruth's life and dramatic career and records the history of baseball in Maryland.

Spreading over 674 acres (273 hectares), Baltimore's Druid Hill Park is one of the largest city parks in the nation. The park is like a vast playground, with bicycle paths, picnic areas, and tennis courts. The Baltimore Zoo, a natural-history museum, and a conservatory are all located within the park.

Among Baltimore's most popular attractions is the renovated Inner Harbor, dominated by Harborplace, a waterfront bazaar of shops and restaurants. Anchored in the harbor is the United States

Baltimore has one of the world's largest natural harbors.

frigate *Constellation*. Commissioned in 1797, the *Constellation* is America's oldest frigate.

Not far from the Inner Harbor, Fort McHenry watches over the city as it did during the War of 1812. Visitors to the fort can explore the restored commander's quarters and examine a collection of early American weapons. Ever since a presidential proclamation was issued in 1948, the American flag has flown above Fort McHenry twenty-four hours a day.

SOUTHERN MARYLAND

Charles, Calvert, and St. Marys counties form a broad peninsula between the Potomac River and Chesapeake Bay. This low-lying region is often referred to as southern Maryland. Between 1949 and 1968, slot machines were legal in Maryland, and gambling became the biggest industry in this part of the state. At the height

Historic St. Mary's City includes a reconstruction of Maryland's first state house.

of the gambling era, Charles County claimed 2,350 slot machines, one for every thirteen residents.

Tobacco is a major cash crop in southern Maryland. Here and there along the highways stand tobacco barns where the leaves are dried, or "cured," before they can be sold. Tobacco auctions are held in such towns as Waldorf, La Plata, and Hughesville from April through June.

A 40-foot (12-meter) cross on St. Clements Island marks the site where the passengers from the *Ark* and the *Dove* first set foot on Maryland soil in 1634. At this spot, Governor Leonard Calvert proclaimed religious freedom in the new colony.

A replica of the square-rigged pinnace *Dove* is docked on the St. Mary's River. Historic St. Mary's City is an 800-acre (324-hectare) outdoor history museum that preserves Maryland's first colonial settlement. Within the museum stands the Margaret Brent Memorial, a monument dedicated to the first American woman to demand the right to vote. The park also includes a replica of Maryland's first state house. The restored Godiah Spray Tobacco Plantation demonstrates how tobacco was raised and prepared in colonial times.

The tragic heritage of the Civil War is recalled at Point Lookout State Park at the mouth of the Potomac. During the war, Point Lookout served as a prison for captured Confederate troops. The Confederate cemetery within the park is the final resting place of the hundreds of men who died at the prison.

Calvert Cliffs State Park stretches along 20 miles (32 kilometers) of 150-foot (46-meter) bluffs overlooking Chesapeake Bay. Fossil hunters are invited to search for the remains of ancient plants and animals that have been exposed along the bluffs. At the nearby Calvert Cliffs Nuclear Power Station, dioramas and films explain how nuclear power is generated.

Solomons is home to the University of Maryland's Chesapeake Biological Laboratory. Solomons's Calvert Marine Museum is an excellent place to learn about the ecology and maritime history of the bay.

THE EASTERN SHORE

A journalist visiting Tilghman Island once heard the patrons of a local restaurant burst into rollicking song: "We don't give a damn for the whole state of Maryland! We're from the Eastern Shore!" Separated from the rest of the state by the Chesapeake, the Eastern Shore maintains a sense of distinctness where traditions flourish and the busy world across the bay seems remote.

The seafood industry is the mainstay of the Eastern Shore's economy. Today, most watermen use powerboats as they tong for oysters or trap hard-shell crabs. But a small number of the old-timers still dredge for oysters in the traditional wooden sailboats known as skipjacks. Watermen on different boats communicate with one another by a code of hand signals that evolved generations ago.

The Wye Mill, which once ground flour for George Washington's army, is the oldest operating gristmill in the United States.

One of the most charming Eastern Shore communities is Chestertown on the Chester River. Around the town square stand the courthouse, customs house, and historic White Swan Tavern. Houses dating back to the Revolutionary War overlook the waterfront. Chestertown is the home of Washington College, which presented George Washington with an honorary degree in 1789. Beyond the mouth of the Chester lies Kent Island, where William Claiborne set up his trading post in 1631.

Since 1671, a gristmill has been grinding cornmeal and whole-wheat flour at Wye Mills. Now fully restored, it is the oldest operating gristmill in the United States. Nearby, at Wye Oak State Park, stands the monumental Wye Oak, a white oak that is believed to be more than four hundred years old. In 1941, the Maryland legislature honored the Wye Oak by designating the white oak as the official state tree.

The town of Cambridge on the Choptank River is a center for the canning and shipping of seafood. To the south sprawls the vast Blackwater National Wildlife Refuge, where thousands of Canada geese winter every year. Blackwater is one of the last retreats of the rare Delmarva fox squirrel.

Scenes of the Eastern Shore, including skipjacks and a pleasure craft along Chesapeake Bay (top left) and various views of Ocean City (top right, bottom left, bottom right)

Salisbury, in the heart of Maryland's poultry region, is the biggest town on the Eastern Shore. A highlight of the town is its delightful River Walk Park, a downtown pedestrian arcade along the meandering Wicomico River. The Salisbury Zoological Park ranks as one of the finest small zoos in the nation.

Every fall, hundreds of duck hunters crouch in the marshes around Crisfield, waiting for mallards to come within range. The ferry from Crisfield is the only way to reach the tiny fishing village on Smith Island in Tangier Sound. Smith Island and most of the other islands along the Eastern Shore suffer from severe erosion and are growing steadily smaller year by year.

Off Maryland's short strip of Atlantic coast lies Assateague Island. Assateague and several smaller barrier islands make up the Assateague Island National Seashore, a refuge for nesting shorebirds. According to legend, the wild ponies of Assateague are descended from horses that reached the island during a seventeenth-century shipwreck.

North of Assateague sparkles Maryland's most popular summer resort, Ocean City. Ocean City boasts 12 miles (19 kilometers) of beaches, where vacationers swim, sunbathe, sail, and windsurf. Families stroll along the boardwalk, sampling saltwater taffy and browsing through the souvenir shops. Ocean City sponsors activities throughout the year, including a Bavarian festival each October and the trimming of a giant Christmas tree on the beach in December.

This brief tour can touch upon only a handful of the attractions that make Maryland such a fascinating place to visit. Each town has its legends and historic shrines, and every region has unique annual festivals. With its remarkable diversity, the state of Maryland offers something special for everyone.

FACTS AT A GLANCE

GENERAL INFORMATION

Statehood: April 28, 1788, seventh state

Origin of Name: Named in honor of Queen Henrietta Maria, wife of King Charles I of England

State Capital: Annapolis

State Nickname: Old Line State, Free State

State Flag: Maryland boasts one of the most colorful state flags. The upper left and lower right quadrants each contain the gold-and-black coat of arms of the Calverts. The other two quadrants each display the red-and-white coat of arms of the Crosslands, the family of the first Lord Baltimore's mother.

State Bird: Baltimore oriole

State Flower: Black-eyed Susan

State Tree: White oak

State Dog: Chesapeake Bay retriever

State Boat: Skipjack

State Fish: Rockfish

State Insect: Baltimore checkerspot butterfly

State Sport: Jousting

State Song: "Maryland, My Maryland," words by James R. Randall, sung to the tune of "O Tannenbaum," adopted in 1939:

> The despot's heel is on thy shore,
> Maryland, my Maryland!
> His torch is at thy temple door,
> Maryland, my Maryland!
> Avenge the patriotic gore
> That flecked the streets of Baltimore,
> And be the battle-queen of yore,
> Maryland, my Maryland!

A moment of repose on the day of the Maryland Hunt Cup Race at Snow Hill

POPULATION

Population: 4,216,941, eighteenth among the states (1980 census)

Population Density: 403 people per sq. mi. (156 people per km²)

Population Distribution: Four-fifths of all Marylanders live in or near cities. Most of those urban dwellers call one of two areas home. Baltimore and its suburbs constitute the most populous area for Maryland dwellers. Many others live in suburban counties just north of Washington, D.C.

Baltimore	786,741
Silver Spring	72,893
Dundalk	71,293
Bethesda	63,022
Columbia	52,518
Towson	51,083
Rockville	43,811
Hagerstown	34,132
Bowie	33,695
Annapolis	31,740
Frederick	28,066
Gaithersburg	26,424

Population Growth: Unlike some states that have experienced rapid population booms, Maryland's growth has been steady over the years. The most rapid growth came in the years following World War II, when Washington, D.C., workers and others helped change rural land in Maryland into commuter suburbs.

Year	Population
1790	319,728
1800	341,548
1820	407,350
1840	470,019
1860	687,049
1880	934,943
1900	1,188,044
1920	1,449,661
1940	1,821,244
1950	2,343,001
1960	3,100,689
1970	3,923,897
1980	4,216,941

GEOGRAPHY

Borders: Maryland is bordered by Pennsylvania on the north and Delaware on the east. Virginia, Chesapeake Bay, and West Virginia border Maryland on the south. West Virginia borders Maryland on the west.

Highest Point: Backbone Mountain, 3,360 ft. (1,024 m) above sea level

Lowest Point: Sea level along the coast

Greatest Distances: North to south—124 mi. (200 km)
East to west—238 mi. (383 km)

Area: 10,460 sq. mi. (27,091 km²)

Rank in Area Among the States: Forty-second

Rivers: The majestic yet slow-moving Potomac River forms Maryland's southern boundary with Virginia and West Virginia. It is Maryland's longest and best-known river. Many others flow into Chesapeake Bay. The Susquehanna, which originates in New York, flows into the northern part of the bay. The Severn, Gunpowder, Patapsco, Patuxent, and Wicomico drain the Western Shore. The bay's Eastern Shore contains the Chester, Choptank, Nanticoke, and Pocomoke. The Youghiogheny and several other rivers flow westward from the Appalachian Plateau and join the Ohio River system.

Lakes: Although Maryland is surrounded by rivers, bay, and ocean, it has few large lakes. The largest lake is Deep Creek Lake, which covers 3,900 acres (1,578 hectares) in Garrett County. Other lakes in the state include Prettyboy Reservoir, Liberty Lake, and Triadelphia Reservoir. All are man-made lakes.

Ocean City

Coast: Despite the huge cut made into Maryland by Chesapeake Bay, the state has only 31 mi. (50 km) of coastline along the Atlantic Ocean. However, Maryland has about 3,190 mi. (5,134 km) of coastline along Chesapeake Bay. Chesapeake Bay is the largest inlet in the eastern United States.

Topography: Five main topographical regions cross Maryland: the Appalachian Plateau, the Appalachian Ridge and Valley, the Blue Ridge, the Piedmont, and the Atlantic Coastal Plain. All are parts of larger regions that run from northeast to southwest along the eastern region of the United States.

The Appalachian Plateau, part of the great Appalachian mountain chain that forms the backbone of the eastern United States, touches the northwest corner of Maryland. Backbone Mountain, Maryland's highest point, at 3,360 ft. (1,024 m), lies here. Broad, fertile valleys cut by high ridges mark the Appalachian Ridge and Valley. In Maryland, this region includes the Hagerstown Valley. Farther east lies the Blue Ridge. This scenic section is part of the Blue Ridge Mountains, which extend from Pennsylvania to Georgia. The Piedmont, which contains gently rolling hills, covers the west-central portion of the state. Swift-moving rivers have carried rich limestone soil to the region, making the Piedmont a fertile agricultural area. More than half of Maryland lies within the Atlantic Coastal Plain. This smooth, low-lying region provides soil suitable for cattle farming and for growing fruits, vegetables, and tobacco.

Fresh snow along a creek at Cunningham Falls State Park near Thurmont

Climate: Maryland's climate reflects its position in the middle of the eastern states. Marylanders experience neither the bone-chilling cold of New England nor the constant summer swelter of the South. Yet temperatures have been known to hit extremes in Maryland. The coldest Maryland temperature ever recorded was -40° F. (-40° C), at Oakland on January 13, 1912. The hottest temperature ever recorded was 109° F. (43° C), at Cumberland and Frederick on July 10, 1936.

Maryland, despite its small size, has a notable temperature range between the sometimes muggy coast and the cooler mountains. Coastal Baltimore has an average January temperature of 39° F. (4° C) and an average July temperature of 75° F. (24° C). The western mountain region averages 29° F. (-1.6° C) in January and 68° F. (20° C) in July.

NATURE

Trees: Oak, spruce, hemlock, white pine, maple, hickory, yellow pine, cedar, red gum, cypress, tupelo, ash, black locust, beech, poplar, elm, chestnut

Among the many kinds of wild animals found in Maryland are raccoons (top left), white-tailed deer (top right), and red foxes (bottom).

Wild Plants: Black-eyed Susan, tiger lily, laurel, daisy, rhododendron, blackberry, dewberry, raspberry, wild strawberry, azalea, honeysuckle, sedge

Animals: White-tailed deer, red foxes, gray foxes, raccoons, opossums, skunks, woodchucks, weasels, cottontail rabbits, squirrels, otters, wild ponies, mink, terrapins, bears, king snakes, rattlesnakes, copperheads

Birds: Baltimore orioles, ducks, geese, bald eagles, partridges, woodcocks, grouse, wild turkeys, nuthatches, mockingbirds, cardinals, wrens, titmice, ravens, bluebirds, thrushes, warblers

Fish and Other Marine Life: Bluefish, striped bass (rockfish), menhaden, sea trout, carp, catfish, trout, sucker, pike, clams, oysters, crabs

Birds that nest in Maryland include grouse (left) and bald eagles (above).

GOVERNMENT

Maryland's government, like the federal government, is divided into three branches. The legislative (lawmaking) branch consists of the General Assembly, which meets every year. It has two houses: a 47-member senate, and a 141-member house of representatives. All legislators are elected to four-year terms.

The executive branch enforces the laws. Voters elect the governor, lieutenant governor, attorney general, and comptroller. The governor appoints a secretary of state, adjutant general, and members of various state boards. Executive officials serve four-year terms. The governor may not serve more than two consecutive terms.

Courts form the judicial branch. The seven-member court of appeals is the state's highest court. The next-highest court is the court of special appeals. The governor appoints appeals-court justices, but after serving two years, the justices must be elected. Eight circuit courts and twelve district courts serve the state.

Number of Counties: 23, plus one independent city (Baltimore)

U.S. Representatives: 8

Electoral Votes: 10

EDUCATION

Education has always been important to the people of Maryland. In colonial days, schools were controlled privately. The first free school was King William's School, established by Governor Francis Nicholson in 1696. Legislation providing for a statewide system of public schools was passed in 1826. The legislature created a state board of education and superintendent of public schools in 1864.

Many colleges and universities serve Maryland. The largest state school is the University of Maryland, which has campuses in College Park, Baltimore, Princess Anne, and Catonsville. Other state schools include Morgan State University, Towson State University, and Coppin State College, all in Baltimore; Bowie State University, in Bowie; Frostburg State University, in Frostburg; St. Mary's College of Maryland, in St. Mary's City; and Salisbury State University, in Salisbury.

Johns Hopkins University, with its world-renowned medical school, is Maryland's most noted private university. Others include St. John's College, in Annapolis; Loyola College, St. Mary's Seminary and University, University of Baltimore, Baltimore Hebrew College, Sojourner-Douglass College, and College of Notre Dame of Maryland, all in Baltimore; Goucher College, in Towson; Western Maryland College, in Westminster; Columbia Union College, in Takoma Park; Hood College, in Frederick; Washington College, in Chestertown; Washington Theological Union, in Silver Spring; and Villa Julie College, in Stevenson.

Three other schools deserve special note. The Peabody Conservatory of Music and the Maryland Institute, College of Art, both in Baltimore, enjoy national reputations. The United States Naval Academy in Annapolis produces the navy's future leaders.

ECONOMY AND INDUSTRY

Principal Products:
Agriculture: Poultry, fruits, dairy products, beef cattle, eggs, oats, wheat, corn, tobacco, soybeans, apples, strawberries, cucumbers, hay, snap beans, tomatoes, ornamental trees and shrubs

Manufacturing: Electrical machinery, processed foods, dried spices, chemicals, paints, soap, drugs, cosmetics, fertilizers

Natural Resources: Stone, marble, coal, natural gas, fish and seafood

Business and Trade: Service industries contribute about 80 percent of the gross state product. The federal government is by far the most important employer. The United States Naval Academy, the National Institutes of Health, the Census Bureau, the National Aeronautics and Space Administration, the Social Security Administration, and several military bases are based in Maryland. Also, many Marylanders commute to government jobs in Washington, D.C.

Baltimore is a major import-and-export center. Its port ranks eighth among American ports in annual tonnage. The city also serves as Maryland's center for wholesale and retail trade.

Even though service industries form the most important part of the economy, Maryland is still known for its manufactured goods. Electrical machinery and equipment are the most important manufactured goods.

**Left: The Chesapeake and Delaware Canal
Above: Lumber being loaded onto cargo ships
in Baltimore Harbor**

Communication: Maryland enjoys a reputation for producing quality
newspapers. The state's first paper, the *Maryland Gazette*, first rolled off the presses
in 1727. Today, Maryland has about 80 newspapers, including about 15 dailies. The
nationally renowned Baltimore *Sun* is the largest of these papers.

The state has about 105 AM and FM radio stations and about 15 television
stations. The state's earliest radio stations, WCAO and WFBR, first went on the air
in 1922. WMAR-TV, the state's television pioneer, began telecasting in 1947.

Transportation: Ever since its founding, Baltimore has been one of America's
busiest ports. Ships from Baltimore and Cambridge carry goods throughout the
world.

Maryland's central location makes it a land-transportation hub as well. More
than 27,400 mi. (44,095 km) of roads crisscross the state, including Interstate
highways 70, 83, and 95.

Baltimore has served as a railroad center ever since the Baltimore and Ohio
opened as the first railroad in America to transport both passengers and freight.
About 1,000 mi. (1,609 km) of railroad track run through Maryland.

Maryland has about 135 airports. The largest of these is Baltimore-Washington
International Airport, in the Baltimore suburb of Friendship.

Visitors enjoying a ride at the Carroll County Farm Museum in Westminster

SOCIAL AND CULTURAL LIFE

Museums: Maryland's pride in its cultural heritage is reflected in its fine museums, many of which are located in Baltimore. The city's Peale Museum, one of the oldest art museums in the nation, is now part of a large municipal museum complex known as the Baltimore City Life Museums. Among the other museums included in the complex are the H. L. Mencken House, the Baltimore Center for Urban Archaeology, and the Carroll Mansion. The Maryland Historical Society houses the original manuscript of "The Star-Spangled Banner," as well as Maryland furniture, miniatures, glass, jewelry, and silver. The Baltimore Museum of Art features the largest American public collection of the works of French painter Henri Matisse. The Walters Art Gallery contains art from almost every nation and historical period. The University of Maryland at College Park has a gallery specializing in American works. The Maryland Science Center and the Davis Planetarium provide a fascinating look into the world of science. The B & O Railroad Museum celebrates America's first passenger railroad. The Center for Urban Archaeology allows visitors to watch archaeologists at work identifying recently excavated artifacts.

The Old Line State also has many other specialized museums. In Annapolis, the United States Naval Academy Museum honors that school's proud history. Calvert Marine Museum in Solomons examines local maritime history and marine life. The

Chesapeake Bay Maritime Museum features drawings, models, and examples of the twenty-eight principal types of Chesapeake Bay craft. The Barbara Fritchie House and Museum in Frederick honors the woman who dared Confederate troops to shoot her "old gray head." The Fire Museum of Maryland near Lutherville contains old-time fire-fighting equipment. The Carroll County Farm Museum in Westminster depicts rural life in Maryland in the late 1800s. History House in Cumberland displays a Victorian parlor, library, schoolroom, kitchen, and dining room. Radcliffe Maritime Museum in Baltimore, part of the Maryland Historical Society, has decoys, paintings of clipper ships, and a replica of a nineteenth-century sailor's bunk. The North American Wildfowl Art Museum in Salisbury explores the history and development of decoy carving in America.

Libraries: The first known libraries in Maryland opened in 1692, when ministers supplied three frontier forts with religious books. Seven years later, Reverend Thomas Bray set up a central library in Annapolis and about thirty parish libraries.

A businessman named Enoch Pratt created the library that bears his name in 1886. Today, the Enoch Pratt Free Library in Baltimore remains the largest library in Maryland. The Johns Hopkins University Library contains a large collection of medical books. The Maryland Historical Society has books and manuscripts on the history of Maryland. Maryland State Law Library in Annapolis boasts many rare books, maps, and newspapers. The University of Maryland Library has a large East Asian collection. Other notable libraries include the National Library of Medicine in Bethesda and the Maryland State Library in Annapolis. A good system of county and regional libraries serves the state.

Performing Arts: Baltimore, an economic hub, is also Maryland's cultural center. The Lyric Theater annually hosts the Baltimore Symphony Orchestra, Baltimore Opera, and Baltimore Ballet. The Peabody Conservatory, one of the nation's most respected schools of music, sponsors a variety of musical programs throughout the year. The Morris A. Mechanic Theater and Center Stage Repertory Theater provide drama and comedy for Baltimore theatergoers. The Theater Project brings experimental drama and music to the city.

Sports and Recreation: In baseball, Baltimore is the home of the American League Baltimore Orioles. Many fans think the glorious Oriole teams of the late 1960s and early 1970s were among the best that ever played. The Orioles won World Series championships in 1966, 1970, and 1983. Baltimore is also home to the Baltimore Blast, a Major Indoor Soccer League team.

Until the mid-1980s, the National Football League Baltimore Colts provided Sunday thrills. Hall of Fame quarterback Johnny Unitas and teammates Lenny Moore, Alan Ameche, and Gene "Big Daddy" Lipscomb led the Baltimore team to titles in 1958 and 1959. The Colts also won Super Bowl V in 1971. Owner Robert Irsay moved the team to Indianapolis in 1984.

Lacrosse is a college mania in autumn, when Johns Hopkins and the University of Maryland often battle for the national championship. Maryland has an unusual state sport: jousting. Would-be Sir Lancelots battle each other at summer and autumn festivals.

For many sports fans, Maryland means the Preakness. This second leg of Thoroughbred horse racing's Triple Crown attracts America's finest horses. Those

The Clara Barton House   **The H. L. Mencken House**

who love the outdoors can enjoy Maryland's thirty-three state parks and nine state forests, as well as all the water-related activities that Chesapeake Bay has to offer.

Historic Sites and Landmarks:

Antietam National Battlefield, near Sharpsburg, preserves the site of one of the Civil War's most devastating battles.

Chesapeake and Ohio Canal National Historical Park allows visitors to follow a towpath that extends for 184.5 mi. (297 km) along the historic canal from Cumberland to Washington, D.C.

Clara Barton National Historic Site, in Glen Echo, preserves the home of the founder of the American Red Cross. The house served as the headquarters of the American Red Cross until 1904.

Fort Frederick, near Big Pool, is the last remaining British stone fort in North America. Built in the 1750s, it became the cornerstone of Maryland's frontier defense during the French and Indian Wars.

Fort McHenry National Monument and Historic Shrine, in Baltimore, is the fort that during the War of 1812 inspired Francis Scott Key to write "The Star-Spangled Banner."

Frostburg contains restored and renovated buildings from the years when the town was an important stop on the National Road.

Historic St. Mary's City, near Lexington Park, is a restoration of Maryland's first colonial settlement. It includes the reconstructed 1676 State House, a tobacco plantation reconstruction, archaeological sites, and a replica of the *Dove.*

H. L. Mencken House, in Baltimore, is the one-time residence of the famous journalist. It has been restored with original furnishings and some of Mencken's personal belongings.

William Paca House, in Annapolis, is the restored home of one of Maryland's signers of the Declaration of Independence.

Edgar Allan Poe House, in Baltimore, was where the famous writer lived from 1832 to 1835.

Point Lookout State Park, at the mouth of the Potomac River, is the site of a former prison for captured Confederate soldiers.

Wye Mill, in Wye Mills, is the oldest gristmill in operation in the United States. It is on the National Register of Historic Places.

Other Interesting Places to Visit:

Assateague Island National Seashore, on Assateague Island, has free-roaming wild ponies and a refuge for nesting shorebirds.

Baltimore Zoo, the nation's third-oldest zoo, includes a children's zoo, an African Watering Hole, and more than twelve hundred animals.

Chesapeake Biological Laboratory, on Solomons Island, contains a museum where visitors may learn about the bay's ecology and maritime history.

Cranesville Sub-Arctic Swamp, near Oakland, contains many species of plants ordinarily found in the Arctic. The swamp has been designated a National Natural History Landmark.

Crystal Grottoes Caverns, near Boonsboro, feature fanciful rock formations and peaceful river surroundings.

Harborplace, in Baltimore, is an enclosed collection of stores, restaurants, and theaters in Baltimore's Inner Harbor area.

Maryland State House, in Annapolis, is the nation's oldest state legislative building in continuous use.

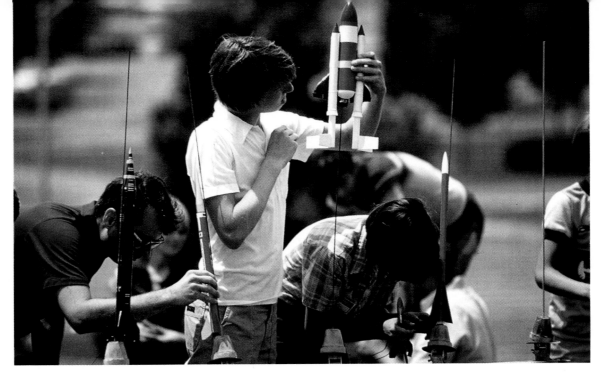

Visitors at the NASA/Goddard Space Flight Center in Greenbelt

NASA/Goddard Visitor Center and Museum, in Greenbelt, shows visitors simulated rocket launches.

National Institutes of Health, in Bethesda, offers a tour of a health-research laboratory.

Ocean City, on Maryland's Atlantic coast, is a popular resort that features beaches, boardwalks, and souvenir shops.

Babe Ruth Birthplace and Baltimore Orioles Museum, in Baltimore, honors baseball great Babe Ruth and the history of baseball in Maryland.

Seton Shrine, in Emmitsburg, honors Elizabeth Ann Seton, the first American-born woman to be named a saint by the Roman Catholic church.

USF Constellation, in Baltimore, built in 1797, was the first frigate built by the United States.

United States Naval Academy, in Annapolis, is one of America's oldest military-service academies.

IMPORTANT DATES

1524—Italian explorer Giovanni da Verrazano is thought to have paused at Chesapeake Bay on his way up the Atlantic coast

122

1608—Captain John Smith reaches Maryland while exploring Chesapeake Bay

1631—Virginian William Claiborne settles Kent Island as a northern extension of Virginia

1632—King Charles I of England grants Cecil Calvert, the second Lord Baltimore, a charter to the Maryland region

1633—Leonard Calvert, brother of the second Lord Baltimore, is appointed governor of the Maryland region; he and a large group of colonists set sail for Maryland in two ships, the *Ark* and the *Dove*

1634—The *Ark* and *Dove* arrive at St. Clements Island; Governor Calvert founds St. Mary's City

1635—Maryland colonists begin farming tobacco

1649—Maryland passes a toleration act granting religious freedom to all Christians; Puritans from Virginia found Providence

1652—The Susquehannock sign a treaty that gives land on the upper Chesapeake Bay to Maryland

1654—Virginia Puritans led by William Claiborne seize control of Maryland

1658—The second Lord Baltimore regains control of Maryland

1664—Slavery becomes sanctioned by law in Maryland

1689—A Protestant group overthrows the third Lord Baltimore's government and demands that the colony come under the direct rule of the British Crown

1691—Royal governors appointed by the British Crown begin ruling the colony

1694—Royal governor Francis Nicholson moves the colonial capital from St. Mary's City to Anne Arundel Town, which he renames Annapolis

1696—King William's School is founded at Annapolis

1715—The Calvert family regains control of Maryland

1727—Maryland's first newspaper, the *Maryland Gazette*, is founded

1729—Baltimore is founded

1732—Maryland cedes more than 3 million acres (1.2 million hectares) of land after border disputes with Pennsylvania and Virginia

1765—Citizens of Annapolis riot against the Stamp Act

The laying out of Baltimore in 1730

1767—Charles Mason and Jeremiah Dixon finish mapping out the boundary between Maryland and Pennsylvania; this boundary line becomes known as Mason and Dixon's Line

1774—As a protest against British oppression, Maryland patriots burn the British vessel *Peggy Stewart* and its cargo of tea

1776—Maryland declares its independence from England and writes its first state constitution

1783—Annapolis becomes the temporary national capital

1784—At the Maryland State House in Annapolis, Americans ratify the Treaty of Paris ending the Revolutionary War

1788—Maryland ratifies the U.S. Constitution and enters the Union as the seventh state

1791—Maryland donates 70 sq. mi. (181 km²) of land on the Potomac River for the permanent U.S. capital—Washington, the District of Columbia

1792—Benjamin Banneker publishes his first almanac

1813—During the War of 1812, the British blockade Chesapeake Bay; British Admiral Sir George Cockburn raids Havre de Grace

1814—Francis Scott Key, watching the bombardment of Baltimore's Fort McHenry, composes the "The Star-Spangled Banner"

1826—The Maryland legislature provides for the establishment of public schools throughout the state; Jews are given the right to vote in Maryland

The first bloodshed of the Civil War occurred when southern supporters assaulted Union troops passing through Baltimore on April 19, 1861.

1828—Construction begins on the Chesapeake and Ohio Canal and on the Baltimore and Ohio Railroad, the first railway system in the United States

1829—Chesapeake and Delaware Canal opens

1830—*Tom Thumb,* the first American-built steam locomotive, makes its first trip, from Baltimore to Ellicott's Mills; the B & O becomes the first American railroad to offer passenger service

1837—Baltimore *Sun* begins publication

1840—The world's first school of dental surgery opens in Baltimore

1844—The world's first telegraph line is built between Baltimore and Washington, D.C.

1845—United States Naval Academy opens at Annapolis

1850—Chesapeake and Ohio Canal is completed from Georgetown to Cumberland

1861—First bloodshed of the Civil War occurs when Maryland residents attack Union troops in Baltimore; President Abraham Lincoln imposes martial law to keep Maryland in the Union

1862—Union forces defeat Confederate forces in the Battle of Antietam, the bloodiest single day of battle in American history

1864—Maryland adopts a third state constitution abolishing slavery

1866—George Peabody founds the first endowed school of music in the United States

1867—Voters adopt a new state constitution

1876—Johns Hopkins University opens

1877—A huge railroad strike originating in Baltimore cripples the nation's rail lines

1881—Baltimore civic leaders found the Charity Organization Society to promote better education and eliminate child labor

1882—Enoch Pratt gives Baltimore a huge sum of money to found a public circulating library

1902—Maryland becomes the first state in the nation to pass a workmen's compensation law

1904—A disastrous fire sweeps Baltimore

1935—A case argued by Thurgood Marshall for the NAACP opens University of Maryland Law School to blacks

1942—Andrews Air Force Base opens; Shangri-La (later renamed Camp David) is established as the official retreat for United States presidents

1952—Chesapeake Bay Bridge (now William P. Lane, Jr., Memorial Bridge), linking the Eastern Shore with the rest of Maryland, opens

1961—Maryland becomes the first state to establish a public agency for historic preservation

1967—Maryland native Thurgood Marshall becomes the first black justice of the U.S. Supreme Court; a constitutional convention meets to write a new state constitution

1968—Maryland native Spiro Agnew is elected vice-president of the United States; riots in Baltimore following the assassination of Martin Luther King, Jr., destroy millions of dollars' worth of property; proposed state constitution is rejected by voters

1972—Maryland voters approve a state lottery

1973—Spiro Agnew resigns as vice-president after pleading no contest to a felony charge

1978—President Jimmy Carter meets at Camp David with Egyptian President Anwar el-Sadat and Israeli Prime Minister Menachem Begin and succeeds in bringing peace between the two Middle Eastern countries

1980—Baltimore's Harborplace, considered a model for urban festival marketplaces, opens

1987—Barbara Mikulski becomes Maryland's first woman U.S. senator; Kurt Schmoke becomes Baltimore's first black mayor

IMPORTANT PEOPLE

Spiro Theodore Agnew (1918-   ), born in Baltimore; politician; governor of Maryland (1967-69); vice-president of the U.S. (1969-73); resigned from office after being charged in a bribery scandal

Benjamin Banneker (1731-1806), born near Ellicott's Mills (now Ellicott City); astronomer, mathematician, surveyor, almanac writer; helped lay out the boundaries of District of Columbia; in 1792, began publishing almanacs bearing his name

Joshua Barney (1759-1818), born in Baltimore; naval officer; served admirably during Revolutionary War; privateer during War of 1812

John Barth (1930-   ), born in Cambridge; writer; often uses Maryland as a setting for his novels, which are known for their humor and surrealistic quality; best-known works include *The Sot-Weed Factor*, a fictional account of the misadventures of Ebenezer Cooke; and *Giles Goat-Boy*

Eubie Blake (1883-1983), born in Baltimore; musician, composer; popularized ragtime music; wrote "I'm Just Wild About Harry" and "Love Will Find a Way"; awarded the Presidential Medal of Freedom (1981)

Edwin Thomas Booth (1833-1893), born near Bel Air; actor; considered one of the finest actors of his era, as well as the greatest Hamlet of his day

John Wilkes Booth (1838-1865), born near Bel Air; actor; brother of Edwin Booth; assassin of President Abraham Lincoln

SPIRO AGNEW

BENJAMIN BANNEKER

127

CECIL CALVERT

CHARLES CARROLL

RACHEL CARSON

FREDERICK DOUGLASS

Franklin Buchanan (1800-1874), born in Baltimore; naval officer; became first superintendent of U.S. Naval Academy (1845-47); commanded the *Germantown* during Mexican War (1847-48); commanded Perry's flagship *Susquehanna* on voyage that opened up Japan to the Western world (1853); Confederate admiral during Civil War

Francis Xavier Bushman (1883-1966), born in Baltimore; actor; appeared in more than four hundred motion pictures during the silent-movie era

Cecilius (Cecil) Calvert (1605?-1675), second Lord Baltimore; colonialist; son of George Calvert; after the death of his father, received a charter of land on upper Chesapeake Bay; founded Maryland Colony; drafted a religious toleration act that was approved by the colonial assembly in 1649

Charles Calvert (1637-1715), third Lord Baltimore; son of Cecilius Calvert; governor of Maryland Colony (1661-75); proprietor of the colony (1675-89)

George Calvert (1580?-1632), first Lord Baltimore; British politician, colonialist; was granted charter to create Maryland colony, which he intended to be a refuge for fellow Roman Catholics, but died before charter was issued

Leonard Calvert (1606-1647), son of George and brother of Cecil Calvert; brought two shiploads of English settlers to Maryland (1634); governor of Maryland Colony (1634-47)

Charles Carroll of Carrollton (1737-1832), born in Annapolis; statesman; Maryland signer of Declaration of Independence; one of Maryland's first U.S. senators (1789-92)

Rachel Louise Carson (1907-1964), writer, environmentalist; taught at University of Maryland (1931-36); wrote *Silent Spring*, which alerted Americans to the dangers of pesticides, and *The Sea Around Us*

Peter Cooper (1791-1883), industrialist, philanthropist; built what became known as the *Tom Thumb*, first American steam locomotive, for B & O Railroad (1830)

Stephen Decatur (1779-1820), born near Berlin; naval officer; noted for stopping attacks by Barbary pirates on American ships

Frederick Douglass (1817-1895), born Frederick Augustus Washington Bailey in Talbot County; writer, abolitionist; born a slave, but escaped to freedom as a young man; lectured and wrote on the evils of slavery; led campaign for abolition and suffrage for blacks; wrote *Narrative of the Life of Frederick Douglass*; published the abolitionist newspaper *North Star* (1847-60); U.S. minister to Haiti (1889-91)

Hugh Latimer Dryden (1898-1965), born in Pocomoke City; physicist; his study of turbulence and wind tunnels led to improved aircraft designs; edited *Journal of Aerospace Sciences*; directed guided-missile program of Bureau of Standards

Cass Elliot (1941-1974), born Ellen Naomi Cohen in Baltimore; singer; gained fame as "Mama Cass," lead singer of the Mamas and the Papas; songs include "Monday, Monday" and "California Dreamin' "

Henry Highland Garnet (1815-1882), born in New Market; clergyman, civil-rights leader; stressed racial pride; founded African Colonization Society, which encouraged black Americans to emigrate to Africa; U.S. minister to Liberia

Daniel Coit Gilman (1831-1908), educator; first president of Johns Hopkins University (1875-1901); led development of the graduate school; helped design Johns Hopkins Hospital and School of Medicine

William Stewart Halsted (1852-1922), physician; conducted the first successful blood transfusion in the United States (1881); professor of surgery at Johns Hopkins (1890-1922); established the nation's first school of surgery; introduced rubber gloves and developed many new surgical techniques, including the use of black-silk sutures

Dashiell Hammett (1894-1961), born in St. Marys County; writer; created "hard-boiled" detectives in such novels as *The Maltese Falcon* and *The Thin Man*

John Hanson (1721-1783), born at Mulberry Grove; statesman; member of Continental Congress (1780); first president of the Congress of Confederation (1781-82)

Eleanora (Billie) Holiday (1915-1959), born in Baltimore; singer; considered the greatest jazz and blues singer of her day; toured with the bands of Artie Shaw and Count Basie; became a cabaret and concert performer; wrote about her life in *Lady Sings the Blues*

Johns Hopkins (1795-1873), born in Anne Arundel County; merchant, banker, philanthropist; founded Johns Hopkins University and Johns Hopkins Hospital

Reverdy Johnson (1796-1876), born in Annapolis; lawyer, statesman; U.S. senator (1845-49, 1863-68); U.S. attorney general (1849-50); helped persuade Maryland legislature to remain in Union during Civil War; supported Thirteenth Amendment, which abolished slavery; U.S. minister to Great Britain (1868-69)

Albert (Al) Kaline (1934-   ), born in Baltimore; professional baseball player; led Detroit Tigers for more than two decades; retired with more than 3,000 hits; became one of the best all-around players in baseball history; elected to Baseball Hall of Fame (1980)

HUGH DRYDEN

DASHIELL HAMMETT

BILLIE HOLIDAY

REVERDY JOHNSON

THURGOOD MARSHALL

H. L. MENCKEN

BARBARA MIKULSKI

ADRIENNE RICH

Francis Scott Key (1779-1843), born in Frederick County; lawyer, author; wrote "The Star-Spangled Banner" after watching the British bombardment of Baltimore's Fort McHenry in 1814

Thurgood Marshall (1908-   ), born in Baltimore; lawyer, jurist; first black associate justice of U.S. Supreme Court (1967-   ); as chief counsel for National Association for the Advancement of Colored People (1938-61), helped inspire much civil-rights legislation; awarded the NAACP's Spingarn Medal (1946)

Luther Martin (1748-1826), lawyer, statesman; first attorney general of Maryland (1778-1805, 1818-22); member of Continental Congress (1785) and Constitutional Convention (1787); defended Aaron Burr against treason charges

James McHenry (1753-1816), patriot, public official; served in Continental army (1775-78); private secretary to General George Washington (1778-80); member of Continental Congress (1783-86); Maryland delegate to Constitutional Convention (1787); U.S. secretary of war (1796-1800)

Henry Louis (H. L.) Mencken (1880-1956), born in Baltimore; journalist, writer, social critic; literary critic (1908-24) and coeditor (1914-24) of the magazine *Smart Set*; founder and editor of the magazine *American Mercury* (1924-33); poked fun at American life in his Baltimore *Sun* columns; wrote a number of books, including a linguistic study, *The American Language*

Barbara Mikulski (1936-   ), born in Baltimore; politician; first woman U.S. senator from Maryland (1987-   )

Charles Willson Peale (1741-1827), born in Queen Annes County; artist; one of the leading American artists of his era; painted portraits of many leading Revolutionary figures; founded Peale Museum (1786)

William Pinkney (1764-1822), born in Annapolis; statesman; known as a talented orator and one of the shrewdest interpreters of the Constitution; U.S. minister to Great Britain (1807-11); U.S. attorney general (1811-14); U.S. representative (1815-16); U.S. minister to Russia (1816-18); U.S. senator (1819-22)

Edgar Allan Poe (1809-1849), writer; lived in Baltimore during the early years of his career; created macabre, depressing stories and characters; wrote such poems as "The Raven" and "The Bells" and such stories as "The Pit and the Pendulum" and "The Tell-Tale Heart"

Enoch Pratt (1808-1896), industrialist; endowed Baltimore's Enoch Pratt Free Library, one of the nation's finest public libraries

Adrienne Rich (1929-   ), born in Baltimore; poet; discussed revolutionary change in politics, society, and the self; won 1974 National Book Award for *Diving into the Wreck*

Cal Ripken, Jr. (1960-   ), born in Havre de Grace; professional
baseball player; played more than one thousand consecutive
games as shortstop for Baltimore Orioles; won American League
Most Valuable Player award in 1983

George Herman (Babe) Ruth (1895-1958), born in Baltimore;
baseball player; considered by many to be the greatest player in
baseball history; set major-league records for home runs and runs
batted in and even set a World Series pitching record; hit a record-
setting 60 home runs in 1927; held the record for most home runs
in a career (714) until 1974; had a lifetime batting average of .342;
one of first five players elected to Baseball Hall of Fame (1936)

BABE RUTH

William Donald Schaefer (1921-   ), born in Baltimore;
politician; mayor of Baltimore (1971-87); won nationwide
acclaim for his role in rejuvenating Baltimore; established
Harborplace and Inner Harbor; governor (1987-   )

Raphael Semmes (1809-1877), born in Charles County; naval
officer; as a Confederate officer, singlehandedly disrupted U.S.
Merchant Marine; wrote best-selling memoirs after the Civil War

Elizabeth Ann Bayley Seton (1774-1821), first native-born
American to be canonized by Roman Catholic church; founded a
religious community, the Sisters of Charity of St. Joseph;
established a boarding school and day school for orphans and the
destitute

UPTON SINCLAIR

Upton Beall Sinclair (1878-1968), born in Baltimore; writer; best
known for his muckraking book *The Jungle,* which led to reforms
in America's meat-packing industry

Raymond Ames Spruance (1886-1969), born in Baltimore; naval
officer; defeated Japanese forces at Battle of Midway; led invasion
of Marshall and Caroline islands; led amphibious invasion of
Okinawa and Iwo Jima; U.S. ambassador to the Philippines
(1952-55)

ROGER TANEY

Roger Brooke Taney (1777-1864), born in Calvert County; lawyer,
jurist; U.S. attorney general (1831-33); U.S. secretary of the
treasury (1833-34); chief justice of U.S. Supreme Court (1836-64);
helped Andrew Jackson establish modern Democratic party;
known for upholding federal authority over state authority

Harriet Tubman (1820?-1913), born Araminta Ross in Dorchester
County; abolitionist; escaped from slavery (1849); became a
leading abolitionist who helped more than three hundred other
slaves escape via the Underground Railroad

Anne Tyler (1941-   ), author; lives in Baltimore; noted works
include *Dinner at the Homesick Restaurant, The Accidental Tourist,*
and *Breathing Lessons,* for which she won the 1989 Pulitzer Prize in
fiction

ANNE TYLER

LEON URIS

Leon Uris (1924-   ), born in Baltimore; writer; wrote epic novels dealing with heroes in turbulent nations; best-known works include *Exodus*, *Trinity*, and *Topaz*

Mason Locke Weems (1759-1825), born in Anne Arundel County; author, clergyman; preached that reading good books leads to a good life; wrote a biography of George Washington that introduced the legend that young Washington chopped down a cherry tree

GOVERNORS

Thomas Johnson	1777-1779	Thomas Watkins Ligon	1854-1858
Thomas Sim Lee	1779-1782	Thomas Holliday Hicks	1858-1862
William Paca	1782-1785	Augustus W. Bradford	1862-1866
William Smallwood	1785-1788	Thomas Swann	1866-1869
John Eager Howard	1788-1791	Oden Bowie	1869-1872
George Plater	1791-1792	William Pinkney Whyte	1872-1874
James Brice (acting governor)	1792	James Black Groome	1874-1876
Thomas Sim Lee	1792-1794	John Lee Carroll	1876-1880
John H. Stone	1794-1797	William T. Hamilton	1880-1884
John Henry	1797-1798	Robert M. McLane	1884-1885
Benjamin Ogle	1798-1801	Henry Lloyd	1885-1888
John F. Mercer	1801-1803	Elihu E. Jackson	1888-1892
Robert Bowie	1803-1806	Frank Brown	1892-1896
Robert Wright	1806-1809	Lloyd Lowndes	1896-1900
Edward Lloyd	1809-1811	John Walter Smith	1900-1904
Robert Bowie	1811-1812	Edwin Warfield	1904-1908
Levin Winder	1812-1816	Austin L. Crothers	1908-1912
Charles Ridgely, of Hampton	1816-1819	Phillips Lee Goldsborough	1912-1916
Charles Goldsborough	1819	Emerson C. Harrison	1916-1920
Samuel Sprigg	1819-1822	Albert C. Ritchie	1920-1935
Samuel Stevens, Jr.	1822-1826	Harry W. Nice	1935-1939
Joseph Kent	1826-1829	Herbert R. O'Conor	1939-1947
Daniel Martin	1829-1830	William Preston Lane, Jr.	1947-1951
Thomas King Carroll	1830-1831	Theodore R. McKeldin	1951-1959
Daniel Martin	1831	J. Millard Tawes	1959-1967
George Howard	1831-1833	Spiro T. Agnew	1967-1969
James Thomas	1833-1836	Marvin Mandel	1969-1977
Thomas W. Veazey	1836-1839	Blair Lee III (acting governor)	1977-1979
William Grason	1839-1842	Harry R. Hughes	1979-1987
Francis Thomas	1842-1845	William Donald Schaefer	1987-
Thomas G. Pratt	1845-1848		
Philip Francis Thomas	1848-1851		
Enoch Louis Lowe	1851-1854		

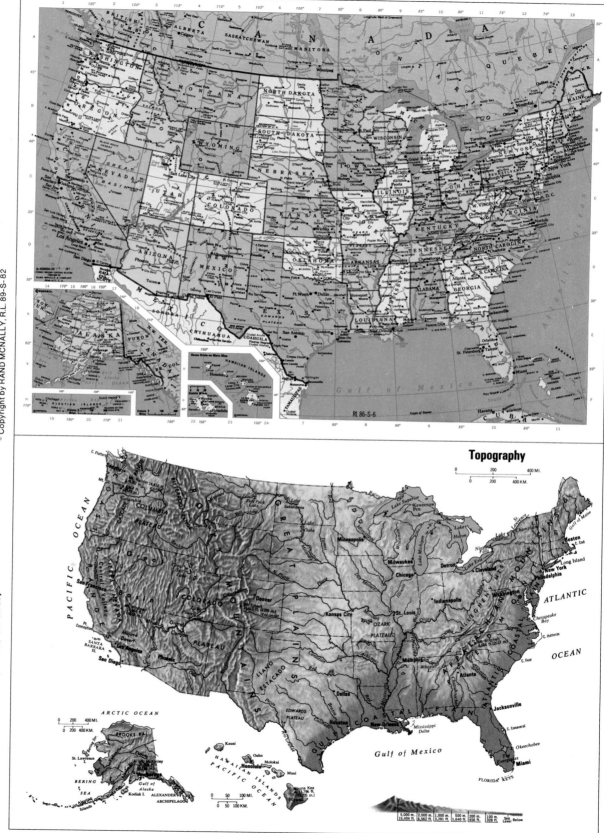

Topography

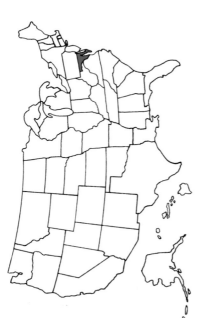

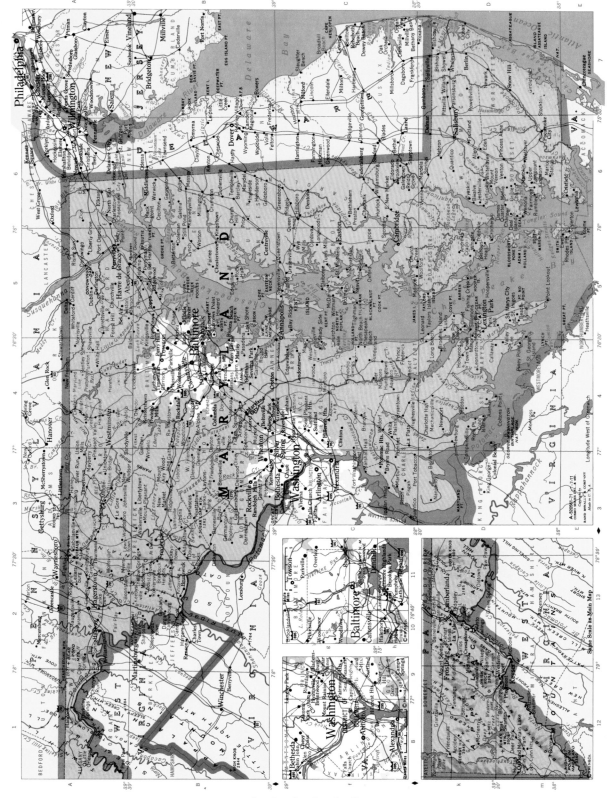

Statute Miles 5 0 5 10 15 20

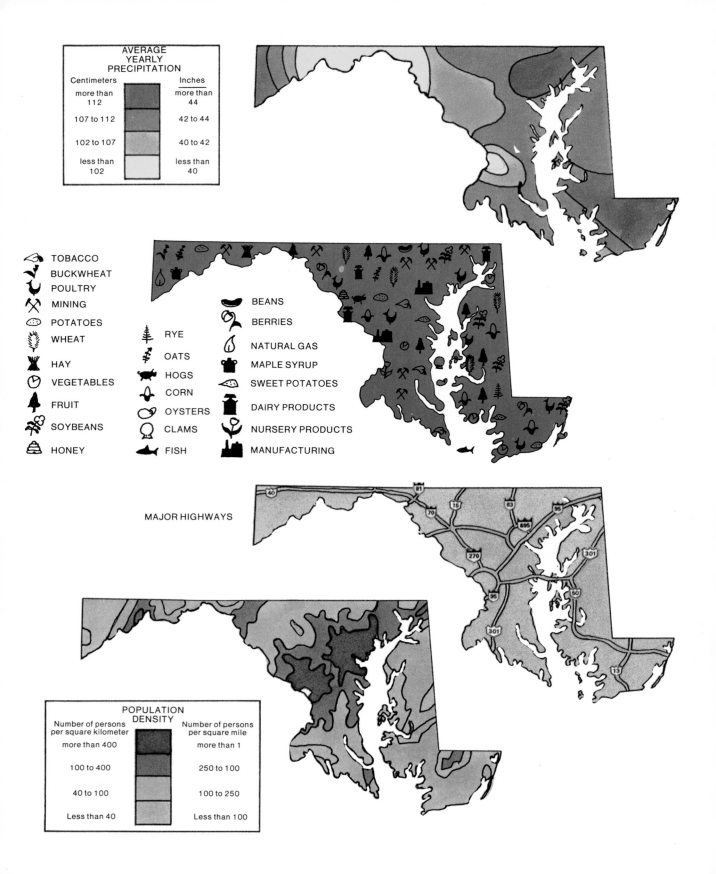

AVERAGE
YEARLY
PRECIPITATION

Centimeters		Inches
more than 112		more than 44
107 to 112		42 to 44
102 to 107		40 to 42
less than 102		less than 40

TOBACCO
BUCKWHEAT
POULTRY
MINING
POTATOES
WHEAT
HAY
VEGETABLES
FRUIT
SOYBEANS
HONEY

RYE
OATS
HOGS
CORN
OYSTERS
CLAMS
FISH

BEANS
BERRIES
NATURAL GAS
MAPLE SYRUP
SWEET POTATOES
DAIRY PRODUCTS
NURSERY PRODUCTS
MANUFACTURING

MAJOR HIGHWAYS

POPULATION
DENSITY

Number of persons per square kilometer		Number of persons per square mile
more than 400		more than 1
100 to 400		250 to 100
40 to 100		100 to 250
Less than 40		Less than 100

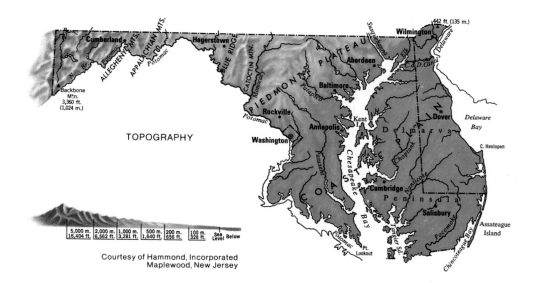

TOPOGRAPHY

Courtesy of Hammond, Incorporated
Maplewood, New Jersey

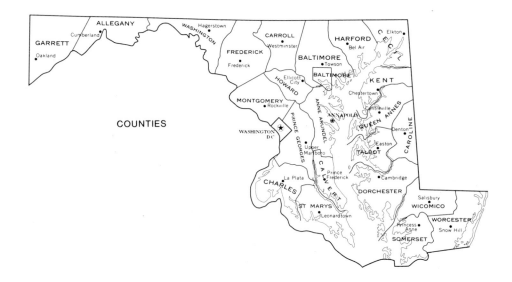

COUNTIES

Ocean racers competing in a boat race on the Chesapeake south of Annapolis

INDEX

Page numbers that appear in boldface type indicate illustrations

140

Laurel Race Course in Prince Georges County

Picture Identifications
Front Cover: Early twentieth-century frame houses in Annapolis
Back Cover: The National Aquarium in Baltimore at night
Pages 2-3: Sailboats participating in a Wednesday-night race sponsored by the Annapolis Yacht Club
Page 6: Black-eyed Susans, the Maryland state flower
Pages 8-9: Maryland farm scene
Pages 20-21: Montage of Maryland residents
Page 26: Detail from a painting by Gerard Soest showing Cecil Calvert, the second Lord Baltimore, handing the map of Maryland to his grandson
Pages 42-43: Detail from Nicolino Calyo's 1836 painting *A View of the Port of Baltimore*
Page 58: A 1926 photograph of the shucking department at the W. H. Killian Company, an oyster-packing company in Baltimore
Page 70: The Maryland State House in Annapolis
Page 80: A participant in a jousting tournament
Pages 90-91: Hooper Strait Lighthouse
Page 108: Montage showing the state flag, the state tree (white oak), state dog (Chesapeake Bay retriever), state bird (Baltimore oriole), and state flower (Black-eyed Susan)

About the Author

Deborah Kent grew up in Little Falls, New Jersey, and received her B.A. in English from Oberlin College. She earned an M.A. in Social Work from the Smith College School of Social Work, and worked for several years at the University Settlement House in New York City. For five years she lived in San Miguel de Allende, Mexico, where she wrote her first novel for young adults.

Deborah Kent is the author of a dozen young-adult novels as well as several titles in the *America the Beautiful* series. She lives in Chicago with her husband and their daughter Janna.

Picture Acknowledgments

Front cover, 2-3, © **Kevin Fleming**; 4, © **Bob Willis**; 5, © **Cameramann International, Ltd.**; 6, © Michael Clemmer/**Photo Options**; 8-9, 11, © **Joe Clark**; 12 (two photos), © **Tom Dietrich**; 13 (right), © **Joe Clark**; 14, © Chesapeake Bay Foundation/**Photri**; 15, © **Tom Dietrich**; 16, © **Jeff Greenberg**; 17, ©Lani Howe/**Photri**; 18, © E. Drifmeyer/**Photri**; 19, © **Kevin Fleming**; 20 (top left), © **Tom Dietrich**; 20 (top right), © **Bob Krist**; 20 (middle left), © **Kevin Fleming**; 20 (bottom left), © **Bob Willis**; 20 (bottom right), © **Porterfield/Chickering**; 21 (top left), © **Kevin Fleming**; 21 (top right), © David Kreider/**Photo Agora**; 21 (bottom left), © Bill Howe/**Photri**; 21 (bottom right), © **Jeff Greenberg**; 23 (left), © Ed Malles/**Photo Options**; 23 (right), © **Bob Krist**; 25, © **Virginia Grimes**; 26, **Enoch Pratt Free Library, Baltimore, MD**; 28, **Maryland Historical Society**; 30, **SuperStock International**; 31, **Maryland Historical Society**; 33, © **Kevin Fleming**; 34, 35, **Historical Pictures Service, Chicago**; 36 (left), © Bill Howe/**Photri**; 36 (right), © Lani Howe/**Photri**; 39, **North Wind Picture Archives**; 41, © Doris DeWitt/**TSW-Click/Chicago Ltd.**; 42-43, **The Baltimore Museum of Art: Purchased by the Women's Committee from funds derived from the 60th Anniversary Ball**; 45, **Historical Pictures Service, Chicago**; 46 (top left), **North Wind Picture Archives;** 46 (bottom left), **Historical Pictures Service, Chicago**; 46 (right), 49, (top left), **Maryland Historical Society**; 49 (top right), © Tom Dietrich/**TSW-Click/Chicago Ltd.**; 49 (bottom), **Historical Pictures Service, Chicago**; 52, **The Bettmann Archive**; 55, 56, **AP/Wide World Photos**; 58, **Maryland Historical Society**; 61 (left), © **Joan Dunlop**; 61 (top right), **The Bettmann Archive**; 61 (bottom right), **Historical Pictures Service, Chicago;** 62, **North Wind Picture Archives**; 63, **The Bettmann Archive**; 65, 66, 67, **AP/Wide World Photos**; 68, © Michael Althaus/**Maryland Tourism Office**; 70, © Bill Howe/**Photri**; 72 (left), © **Tom Dietrich**; 72 (right), © Jim Pickerell/**TSW-Click/Chicago Ltd.**; 73, © Tim McCabe/**Journalism Services**; 74, © **Kevin Fleming**; 75, © **Joe Clark**; 77 (top left), **Maryland Tourism Office**; 77 (top right), © Ralph Roseman/**Photo Options**; 77 (bottom), © **Kevin Fleming**; 78, © **Cameramann International, Ltd.**; 79, © **Photri**; 80, © Dr. Joe Atchison/**Photri**; 83 (left), © **Bob Willis**; 83 (right), **North Wind Picture Archives**; 85, **Maryland Historical Society**; 86, © **Joan Dunlop**; 88 (left), **Maryland Tourism Office**; 88 (right), © Nick Sebastion/**Photri**; 89, © **Bob Willis**; 90-91, © **Bob Krist**; 93, © **Tom Dietrich**; 93 (map), **Len W. Meents**; 94, © Dave Carter/**Photri**; 96 (left), © Mark E. Gibson/**The Marilyn Gartman Agency**; 96 (right), © **Kevin Fleming**; 96 (map), **Len W. Meents**; 98, © **Kevin Fleming**; 99, © **Tom Dietrich**; 100 (left), © R. Krubner/**H. Armstrong Roberts**; 100 (right), © **Porterfield/Chickering**; 102, © James Blank/**Root Resources**; 103, **Shostal Associates/SuperStock;** 103 (map), **Len W. Meents**; 105, © **Bob Krist**; 105 (map), **Len W. Meents**; 106 (top left), © Steve Uzzell/**Root Resources**; 106 (top right), © R. Krubner/**H. Armstrong Roberts**; 106 (bottom left), © **Kevin Fleming**; 106 (bottom right), © Pat Abramson/**Photo Options**; 108 (tree), **SuperStock International**; 108 (butterfly), © Gay Bumgarner/**TSW-Click/Chicago Ltd.**; 108 (flag), **Courtesy Flag Research Center, Winchester, Massachusetts 01890**; 108 (dog), © **Bob Willis**; 108 (bird), © Robert Dunning/**Photri**; 108 (flower), © M.L. Dembinsky, Jr./**M.L. Dembinsky Jr. Photography Assoc.**; 110, © Steve Uzzell/**Root Resources**; 112, © **Kevin Fleming**; 113, © **Tom Dietrich**; 114 (top left), © Jean Reuther/**M.L. Dembinsky Jr. Photography Assoc.**; 114 (bottom), © Rod Planck/**M.L. Dembinsky Jr. Photography Assoc.**; 114 (top right), 115 (left), © Carl L. Sams, II/**M.L. Dembinsky Jr. Photography Assoc.**; 115 (right), © Stan Osolinski/**M.L. Dembinsky Jr. Photography Assoc.**; 117 (left), © **Jeff Greenberg**; 117 (right), © **Porterfield/Chickering**; 118, © Steve Uzzell/**Root Resources**; 120 (left), © **Bob Willis**; 120 (right), © A. Bolesta/**H. Armstrong Roberts**; 122, © Steve Uzzell/**Root Resources**; 124, **North Wind Picture Archives**; 125, **The Bettmann Archive**; 127 (two photos), 128 (Calvert, Carson, Douglass), **Historical Pictures Service, Chicago**; 128 (Carroll), **Maryland Historical Society**; 129 (Dryden, Hammett, Holiday), **AP/Wide World Photos**; 129 (Johnson), 130 (Marshall, Mencken), **Historical Pictures Service, Chicago**; 130 (Mikulski, Rich), 131 (Ruth, Sinclair, Tyler), **AP/Wide World Photos**; 131 (Taney), **Historical Pictures Service, Chicago**; 132, **AP/Wide World Photos**; 136 (maps), **Len W. Meents**; 138, © Steve Uzzell/**Root Resources**; 141, © John McCauley/**Photri**; Back cover, © Dave Carter/**Photri**